The Institute of
Studies in Biolo

Biological Fuels

**This book is to be returned on or before
the last date stamped below.**

LIBREX

*Biology Dept.
King George V College*

First published 1983
by Edward Arnold (Publishers) Limited
41 Bedford Square, London WC1 3DQ

ISBN 0-7131-2864-X

Printed and bound in Great Britain at
The Camelot Press Ltd, Southampton

General Preface to the Series

Because it is no longer possible for one textbook to cover the whole field of biology while remaining sufficiently up to date, the Institute of Biology proposed this series so that teachers and students can learn about significant developments. The enthusiastic acceptance of 'Studies in Biology' shows that the books are providing authoritative views of biological topics.

The features of the series include the attention given to methods, the selected list of books for further reading and, wherever possible, suggestions for practical work.

Readers' comments will be welcomed by the Education Officer of the Institute.

1983   Institute of Biology
                                                20 Queensbury Place
                                                London SW7 2DZ

Preface

How can biology play its part in meeting the world's ever-increasing demand for energy? Can photosynthesis, which already supplies almost all man's food and a host of natural organic products, also make a meaningful contribution to our energy needs? If so, what kinds of technologies are involved and what kinds need to be developed for the future?

This small book attempts to provide a realistic assessment of biological energy production systems and thereby go some way to answering these questions.

Today, around 15% of global fuel consumption is in the form of biomass – mostly as wood, livestock waste and agricultural residues, and mostly burnt inefficiently in the rural areas of the Third World. However as the production and consumption of biomass fuels are made more efficient, and as our fossil and fissile (nuclear) reserves become less and less accessible and so more and more expensive, biofuels will assume even greater importance. Ultimately they should become integral components of the post-fossil fuel era, when biological fuel production will be a major growth industry – in more ways than one!

Glasgow, 1983   C.W.L.

Contents

1 Energy from Biomass — a general introduction

1.1 Bioenergy today

Bioenergy is solar energy captured by green plants through photosynthesis and then stored chemically, usually as carbohydrate. The term is also used to include the chemical energy of fuels derived from primary biomass via a conversion process such as fermentation to alcohol. The annual primary productivity of plants on the Earth is estimated at 100–125 billion tonnes of dry organic matter on land and 44–55 billion tonnes in the oceans. The energy content of this biomass is over 200 times the present annual global energy consumption. Cellulose is the major end-product of photosynthesis, most of which remains un-utilized by man. It therefore represents a large renewable potential source of chemicals and energy.

Cellulose, in the forms of wood and agricultural residues such as straw, historically met virtually all man's energy needs until the relatively recent discovery of easily extractable coal, oil, and finally uranium, allowed the industrialization of societies into what we now call the Developed World. Fossil and fissile fuels predominate in the Developed World. They provide intensive sources of heat and are thermodynamically much superior to wood and charcoal. The fossil fuels themselves are products of vegetative decay brought about by bacteria in processes beginning some 300 million years ago and still occurring today. But the rate of fossil fuel formation is now much slower than the rate of its combustion – hence the so-called 'energy crisis' in which the world finds itself.

What then is the contribution of energy from biomass in the world of today? How does it compare with coal, natural gas, oil and nuclear energy? Is it really significant?

Table 1 Estimated global primary energy use by fuel.

Primary fuel use	EJ	%
Coal	70	23
Natural gas	49	16
Oil	122	40
Nuclear electricity	3	1
Hydroelectricity	15	5
Bioenergy	46	15

Table 1 shows that biomass supplies around 15% (46 exajoules per year) of the world's energy, but because it is classed as a 'non-commercial' fuel (as opposed to the 'commercial' coal, oil, gas and electricity), it is not well documented in global energy statistics and it is impossible to quantify with any degree of accuracy since most of it is consumed in the rural regions of developing countries. Nonetheless, it is vital to those 2.6 billion people at present eking out an existence in the rural Third World where biomass is the largest provider of energy, and where mass poverty precludes the purchase of oil or coal. Over 80% of the world's consumption of fossil and fissile energy occurs in the Developed World (North America, western Europe, eastern Europe including the Soviet Union, Japan, Australia, New Zealand and South Africa), where only 25% of the global population lives. With population projections of a 50% increase in the Third World and only 12–13% in the Developed World by the year 2000, this imbalance can only become greater. At the present time firewood constitutes 65–70% of the energy supply to the whole of Africa and, in countries like Gambia and Tanzania, 99% of the people are dependent on wood as their principal, and often only, fuel. But even in the industrialized countries biofuels are not negligible; they account for some 15% of Finland's energy usage, 9% of Sweden's, 9% of Greece's, 3–4% of the Soviet Union's and 2% of the huge U.S. consumption.

However, most of the useful energy potential of biomass as currently used is squandered by inefficient conversion methods. Furthermore, overdependence on fuelwood in developing countries has already led to disastrous consequences for the environment, while under many prevailing circumstances bioenergy is not economically competitive with the more conventional fuels. But as the technologies associated with bioenergy supplies improve, and these major drawbacks become avoidable, energy from biomass should assume a greater importance in the post-petroleum future.

1.2   Bioenergy in history

Historians estimate that *Homo erectus* knew how to use fire about 600 000 years ago in China, and until the latter part of the seventeenth century man still relied almost entirely upon the burning of wood and charcoal for his energy needs. The fossil fuels had, with the probable exception of Chinese coal around 1000 B.C., been left undisturbed beneath the Earth's surface until the mining of coal in England and then Germany spawned the Industrial Revolution. Before this time there had been an energy crisis just as unwelcome as today's: a shortage not of oil, but of wood. Indeed, the fuelwood crisis of some developing countries in the 1980s is a repetition of a fuelwood crisis of the 1560s in England.

The quadrupling of oil prices by the OPEC cartel in 1973/4 matched the quadrupling of firewood prices in England between 1540 and 1580 – a price rise exerted by market forces and much above the general rate of inflation. Burgeoning industry was the root cause of the wood shortage, and the clearance of the forests in the Scottish Highlands to provide the charcoal for the smelting of iron aroused the most passionate hostility. However, while industry prospered in the rapidly expanding urban areas, the rural poor were driven to desperate measures to obtain their fuel. In northern Britain peat was the answer for those who could afford nothing else. Peat is a feasible alternative to wood and coal where it occurs in large enough quantities, but there was no such resource for people in the East Midlands and central-southern England who were reduced to burning cow-dung cakes for heat, much to the detriment of the soil where formerly dung was the sole fertilizer. Again a parallel can be seen between seventeenth century England and twentieth century India, for example. The fuel crisis was resolved with the advent of coal mining and the price of wood and charcoal stabilized again around 1660.

The environmental consequences of clearing so much forest area in England and the Scottish Highlands are probably incalculable, but the destruction of natural habitats on such a massive scale can only have harmed wildlife in particular and the landscape in general. Yet even after the coal age was well under way in the West, wood remained the predominant fuel in most countries. In the United States for instance wood was pre-eminent until about 1875, and, a generation earlier, it had accounted for over 90% of the national energy consumption. Globally, annual fuelwood use is estimated to have more than doubled in the 40 years up to 1950, after which it has levelled off at about 1070 million m^3. This may be an overestimate but it still means that on a per capita basis consumption is actually decreasing as the world's population inexorably grows.

The disparity in fuel use between the West and most of the rest of the world is illustrated by the fact that just before the Industrial Revolution wood made up at least 40%, and probably much more, of the world's energy usage, while today it is barely 15%; but this 15% is largely consumed by over 90% of the population of the Third World.

Although solid biomass fuels like wood have had most impact in the past, liquid fuels such as alcohol have also been recognized from ancient times. Alcoholic fermentation is mentioned in the *Old Testament Book of Genesis* (Chapter 9, 21), and variations on the brewing process were chronicled in civilized Egypt and Mesopotamia (modern Iraq and Syria) two and a half thousand years before Christ. Ethanol production via the fermentation of various grains and fruits in particular has continued down through the centuries. However, for the moment we are most interested in the use of alcohol as a fuel rather than as a potable liquor. The two main alcohols are methanol, CH_3OH and ethanol, C_2H_5OH. It is important to distinguish between them, not just for drinking purposes, but because they are produced by entirely different methods. Ethanol is a product of the microbial fermentation of biomass, while methanol arises from the thermal decomposition of dry biomass under conditions of limited oxygen availability; the methanol is then synthesized from the resulting mixture of carbon monoxide and hydrogen (synthesis gas):

$$CO + 2H_2 \rightarrow CH_3OH.$$

Table 2 Biomass alcohol use since 1830.

Year	Event
1830	Methanol replaced malodorous fish and whale oils for lighting
1850s	Methanol, distilled from wood, used by Parisians for cooking, heating and lighting
1890	Ethanol employed for the first time as a motor fuel
1900s	3–4 hp ethanol engines common in Germany
1914–18	Wood burners used by French and Germans in many vehicles, including aeroplanes and tanks, to produce a powering mixture of alcoholic gases, hydrogen, and carbon monoxide
	Commercial wood hydrolysis processes giving rise to fermentable sugars for ethanol manufacture developed by Germans
1915	Ethanol produced commercially via sawdust hydrolysis and fermentation in Louisiana and South Carolina
1920s	Brazilians experiment with ethanol fermented from sugar-cane to power four-cycle combustion engines
1923	Neat ethanol fuels motor cars in races at Rio de Janeiro
1930s	Almost all U.S. ethanol fermented from grain and molasses
	Company in north-eastern Brazil sells automobile fuel mixture of 75% ethanol from sugar-cane and 25% ether
	Ethanol fuel exempt from all taxes and restrictions in the U.K.
	U.S. Chrysler Motor Corporation exports 100% ethanol-driven cars to New Zealand
	25% ethanol/75% petrol cars found in Argentina, Australia, Brazil, Cuba, Japan, New Zealand, the Philippines, South Africa and Sweden
1931	Law passed in Brazil to force the blending of ethanol 5%, with imported petrol 95%, in motor vehicles
1939	European alcohol fuel consumption reaches half a million tonnes per annum
1939–45	German road vehicles run on potato-fermented ethanol
	Over 20 plants in western Europe constructed to hydrolyse wood wastes for ethanol fermentations
	Ethanol fermented and distilled in Omaha, Nebraska for U.S. Army. Output rises six-fold in six years
1956	Law passed in Brazil to force the blending of ethanol 10%, with imported petrol 90%, deemed the optimum blend
1962	Grain fermentations account for 22% of U.S. industrial ethanol production – mostly from grain surpluses or damaged crops in the Mid-west
1971	The American state of Nebraska establishes programme to develop the grain alcohol industry – out of which comes 'gasohol': 10% ethanol, 90% unleaded gasoline (petrol)
1975	Brazil launches a National Alcohol Programme to reduce its oil import bill. Sugar-cane and cassava plantations are to be used and over 200 distilleries need to be constructed
1978	First commercial cassava fuel alcohol plant begins operation in Brazil
1980	Motor cars introduced into West Germany running on 15% methanol and 85% petrol

Both alcohols can of course be synthesized from organic chemical feedstocks not derived from biomass at all.

Table 2 charts the history of ethanol and methanol as biofuels, and although not exhaustive, it pinpoints some of the developments of biologically produced alcohols over some 150 years. Methanol and ethanol derived from biomass have both had to compete with the products of synthetic chemical processes over the years. In 1921 the Haber process was patented whereby methanol could be synthesized from carbon monoxide and hydrogen much more cheaply than by the destructive distillation of wood. Similarly, following World War II, the abundance of cheap oil meant that petrochemical ethanol superseded biomass ethanol in many countries. By 1950 the grain alcohol industry in the United States had virtually disappeared. However, as Table 2 shows, biomass alcohols have made a comeback, due to the firm stand taken by OPEC and to the desire of countries such as Brazil to reduce their dependence on ever more expensive oil imports.

Finally, we come to the development of gaseous fuel production, specifically the bacterial anaerobic digestion of biomass to biogas: a mixture of roughly two parts by volume methane and one part carbon dioxide. The phenomenon of inflammable marsh gas arising from the decomposition of organic matter under airless conditions has been recognized for millennia. In the eleventh century B.C. a Chinese historian recorded 'fire in the marsh', and two thousand years ago people in Sichuan, China used this 'natural gas' for salt extraction. Anaerobic digestion was subsequently applied to stabilize and humify the sludge produced in the treatment of organic wastes within septic tanks towards the end of the nineteenth century. In 1895, methane evolving from a septic tank in the city of Exeter was used for street lighting, and this was followed up in the 1920s when several kinds of digesters were built to generate gas. In 1911 the world's first large-scale anaerobic digestion plant to stabilize the sewage sludge produced by the one million inhabitants of Birmingham was built, and subsequently a gas engine generator was added to convert the methane into electricity for light and heat. This was the forerunner of several of the larger sewage works operating today which recycle their gaseous output to help power the plant. A few farms in France and Germany also used cattle dung as a substrate to provide gaseous fuel for cooking during both World Wars. Methane was produced from urban refuse in the U.S.A. in the 1930s and was used as an automobile fuel in Algeria, France, and Germany in World War II.

There is now a re-awakening to the potential of biogas and there are today countless examples of, generally small-scale, on-site digesters producing gas for heat, mechanical power and electricity generation in many countries.

The above examples refer mostly to Western systems of biogas generation but it is in the developing countries where the impact of biogas has the greatest potential, especially in regions of high cattle density. India was the pioneering country in this and a programme of research and development into cow-dung fermentations was initiated in New Delhi in the late 1930s. This gave rise to the family-sized Gobar gas plants introduced by the Khadi Village Industries Commission (KVIC) in 1954, and later to the Gobar Gas Research Station in

1961. The word 'gobar' means cow-dung in Hindi, and the impetus for the development of these plants came from concern over the loss of fertilizer caused by the burning of dung for energy. This problem is overcome in a biogas plant where the residual sludge retains the original nitrogen, phosphorus and potassium following the liberation of the gas, and this soil conditioner can then be applied to the fields. Over 75 000 family-sized units were operating in India by 1979 and the Government hoped, perhaps optimistically, to establish a further half million by 1983, along with a few larger community digesters to cater for the energy needs of whole villages. In mainland China approximately one million units were installed each year over a seven year period up to 1978, mainly in Sichuan Province. Other countries too have recently been very active in this sphere.

1.3 Terms and definitions

There has recently appeared in the literature a number of relatively new terms which need to be defined at the outset. These include the following:

Bioenergy is solar energy captured during plant photosynthesis and stored chemically, usually as carbohydrate. The term also refers to the energy content of a fuel derived from biomass (organic plant material) by a conversion process such as fermentation.

Biofuels are fuels derived from biomass. They include primary bioenergy resources such as wood, as well as secondary fuels like ethanol, methanol, and biogas which themselves originate from the bioconversion of primary produced photosynthate.

Biological energy conversion or *bioconversion* is the overall process in which biomass is produced, collected and either converted to; or used as, a fuel. In the strict sense the term refers only to conversions mediated by micro-organisms, such as fermentation to ethanol and anaerobic digestion to methane, but generally the thermochemical conversion routes of gasification and pyrolysis, and the combustion of biomass as a precursor to electricity generation, are also included within this definition.

Biomass residues are the plant remains following agricultural or forestry operations. They generally have an alternative use, or uses, to providing energy, and so incur a positive cost for their utilization as an energy source as well as for collection and transportation.

Biomass wastes are organic materials for which no use has been discovered and which generally incur a cost, both in energy and economic terms, before being returned to the environment. Their use as a bioenergy resource therefore incurs a credit which can be offset against collection, transportation, and bioconversion costs.

Energy farms or *fuel plantations* are areas of land, freshwater, or salt water devoted to the cultivation of *fuel crops* specifically for their energy content.

2 Photosynthesis and Biomass Resources

2.1 Solar energy – from Sun to Earth

Energy radiates from the Sun at a rate of some 10^{26} watts, equivalent to just over 10^{34} joules each year. This enormous energy flux results from multiple collisions of hydrogen ions (protons) within the Sun's central core occurring at temperatures approaching 20 million °C. The Sun is a large natural fusion reactor in which the amalgamation of four protons into one helium nucleus ($4H^1 \rightarrow He^4$) liberates 5×10^{-12} J of energy as very short wave radiation of wavelength about 10^{-2} nm. The frequency of these reactions is so great that 600 million tonnes of helium are formed every second and vast numbers of photons are emitted. A photon is the energy content of a single unit or quantum of light radiation. As these quanta of radiation energy journey outwards towards the surface of the Sun they collide with numerous sub-atomic particles and so lose energy and increase their wavelength. Consequently, at the Sun's surface the entire spectrum of electromagnetic radiation is to be found, from γ-rays through X-rays at 1 nm and on to the ultraviolet, visible light, and infra-red regions, low energy microwaves and beyond to long wavelength radiation of several hundred metres. The temperature at the surface is around 6000°C and roughly 98% of the energy emitted into space is conveyed by radiation of wavelengths between 250 and 3000 nm, with about 50% between 350 nm and 750 nm – the region of photosynthetic activity (Fig. 2–1).

However, only a small fraction of the Sun's emitted radiation reaches the Earth: approximately 3×10^{24} J each year which is 75 times our present total proven fossil fuel reserves. But against this seemingly very promising statistic must be set the diffuse, variable nature of solar energy and its incidence on the Earth at a peak flux of only 1 kW m^{-2}. At a specific location on the Earth's surface the insolation is dependent on latitude, season, time of day, cloud cover, and atmospheric pollution. This in turn has a profound influence upon climate and hence biological primary production. Furthermore, the solar spectrum is modified by the atmosphere. 20% of the original solar radiation is absorbed (mostly UV radiation by the ozone layer), 5% is lost by scattering due to dust particles, water vapour, etc., and 25% is reflected back into space by clouds. Finally, on reaching the Earth's surface 5% of the incident energy is also reflected back.

Although about 43% of the solar energy spectrum is potentially photosynthetically active, only about 60% of this radiation which reaches the Earth's surface is available to photosynthetic organisms since the rest falls on oceans (where only a small fraction can be used), deserts, ice and snow, etc. An annual value of 9×10^{23} J is potentially available for photosynthesis on an annual basis, but only around 3×10^{21} J of this is captured by plants, giving an overall

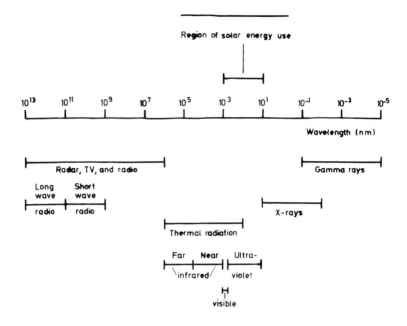

Fig. 2–1 Electromagnetic radiation spectrum.

efficiency of 0.33%. The pattern in which radiation is received during the course of a year varies widely in different parts of the world. The total annual insolation is much less varied. Table 3 shows that England and Wales receive as much as 40% of the annual mean insolation of the most favoured region, the Middle East (Israel). However, while the insolation in equatorial regions is fairly uniform throughout the year at around 20 MJ m^{-2} day, increase in latitude results in increase in seasonal amplitude. Thus the U.K. at about 53°N gleans below 2 MJ m^{-2} day in winter, but over 20 MJ m^{-2} day in high summer. The amount of photosynthesis taking place in the winter months at high latitudes is therefore small.

Figure 2–2 depicts the annual mean global irradiance on a horizontal plane at the Earth's surface in terms of W m^{-2} day. Values of 250 W and above are found principally in the continental desert regions around latitudes 25°N and S, with the amounts of incident energy declining towards both the Equator, due to cloud cover, and the Poles. The Middle East can boast 300 W plus, thus endowing the Arab countries with solar, as well as oil, riches, though of course photosynthesis is limited here due to water and soil nutrient shortages.

Table 3 Insolation in selected countries on horizontal surfaces (MJ m⁻² day)

Location	Latitude	Midsummer mean	Midwinter mean	Annual mean	Midsummer/ midwinter ratio
England and Wales	53°N	18	1.7	8.9	10.6
Central U.S.A.	36°N	26	11	19	2.4
Southern France	44°N	24	5	15	4.8
Israel	33°N	31	11	22	2.8
Australia	30°S	23	13	20	1.8
Japan	40°N	17	7	13	2.4
India	18°N	(26)*	(14)*	30	1.9

*In many parts of India the maximum and minimum insolations occur in April and June respectively, the latter month corresponding with the major monsoon season.

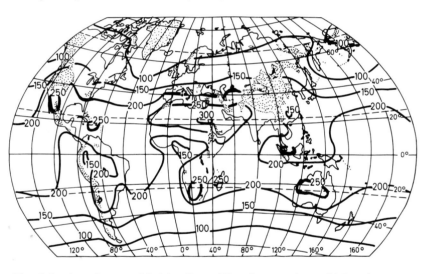

Fig. 2–2 Annual mean global irradiance (W m⁻² averaged over 24 hours) on a horizontal plane at the Earth's surface.

2.2 Photosynthetic mechanisms

Photosynthesis converts solar energy into chemical potential energy, and the fact that the chemical energy is stored makes it valuable to man since it can be tapped as and when required without recourse to large, costly energy storing devices. Most photosynthesis occurs within the chloroplasts of green plant cells and the overall process may be divided into two sets of reactions, the first requiring light and the second not requiring light. They are known as the light and dark reactions, though the latter can occur in both the presence and absence of light. Photosynthesis may be simplified into the equation:

$$CO_2 + 2H_2O + light \rightarrow (CH_2O) + H_2O + O_2$$
carbohydrate

Light energy is absorbed by the chlorophyll and other chloroplast pigments, removing electrons from water molecules and liberating molecular oxygen in a water-splitting reaction. The displaced electrons are conveyed through an electron transport system to reduce pyridine nucleotides to $NADPH_2$ (hydrogenated nicotinamide adenine dinucleotide phosphate).

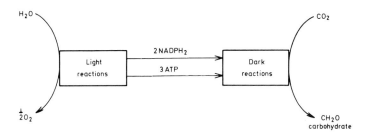

Fig. 2–3   Basic photosynthetic process.

As Fig. 2–3 shows, each CO_2 molecule needs the reducing power of two $NADPH_2$ molecules in the dark phase of carbohydrate formation. Three ATP (adenosine triphosphate) molecules are also required to provide the needed energy. For a more exhaustive treatment of the biochemistry involved the reader is referred to *Studies in Biology no. 37* by Hall and Rao. All plants fix carbon by a 3-carbon cycle involving mainly 3-carbon compound intermediates and most, the so-called C_3 plants, use only this mechanism. These tend to be temperate crops which reach light saturation at a comparatively low intensity of 200–300 J m^{-2} s^{-1}. This is well below the full summer daylight intensity of 800–1000 J m^{-2} s^{-1}, and so most of the radiant energy at high light intensities cannot be utilized by these plants. They also have a temperature optimum in the region of 20°C, which again makes them more suitable for growth in temperate climes.

There are other plants, the 4-carbon or C_4 plants, which utilize an additional synthetic pathway based on 4-carbon compounds. A distinguishing feature of these, mainly tropical species, which include sugar-cane, sorghum, maize and several other grasses, is the presence of two distinct chloroplast types: mesophyll and bundle sheath. C_4 varieties exhibit little or no light saturation, even at intensities of 800 J m^{-2} s^{-1}, and can therefore make better use of high light intensities. Most species also have temperature optima of over 30°C and grow well in conditions of restricted water supply. Whereas C_3 plants transpire 500–700 g of water for every gram of dry matter yield, C_4 plants lose only 250–400 g of water. C_4 species show low photosynthetic activity at 15–20°C however, and are clearly best adapted for tropical environments where their annual biomass productivity invariably exceeds that of C_3 plants grown in temperate regions. C_4 plants also have a low rate of wasteful photorespiration in which the oxidation of carbohydrate to carbon dioxide and water results in no obvious energy benefit to the plant.

Finally, there is a third photosynthetic mechanism adopted by some plants inhabiting arid zones where water conservation is a priority. These species reduce transpiration by keeping their stomata closed during the day and opening them at night when evaporation is less likely to occur. By this simple yet effective expedient photorespiration is also virtually eliminated. These plants perform what is known as Crassulacean Acid Metabolism (CAM). CAM species can colonize deserts but are inevitably slow-growing with limited biomass energy potential. Species vary from cacti to pineapples.

2.3 Photosynthetic efficiency

The efficiency of solar energy capturing systems determines the land area required to collect a given amount of energy. A major factor limiting solar energy conversion by plants is their photosynthetic efficiency. From the simplified photosynthetic equation:

$$CO_2 + 2H_2O + light \rightarrow (CH_2O) + H_2O + O_2$$
$$\text{carbohydrate}$$

where (CH_2O) represents one-sixth of a glucose molecule, the Gibbs free energy(ΔG) stored per mole of CO_2 reduced to glucose is 477 kJ. At least eight quanta of light are required for this reaction, with the usable energy input equivalent to that of monochromatic light of wavelength about 575 nm. Eight quanta of 575 nm light have an energy content of 1665 kJ, giving a maximum photosynthetic efficiency of $477/1665 = 0.286$. The actual efficiency may be less because laboratory experiments have demonstrated that from eight to ten quanta are needed in practice. However, since only light of wavelengths 400–700 nm can be utilized in plant photosynthesis, and this photosynthetically active radiation (PAR) constitutes only about 43% of the total incident solar radiation, the photosynthetic efficiency falls to $0.286 \times 0.43 \times 0.123$.

In land plants the optimally arranged leaf canopy can at most absorb 80% of PAR, while respiration, needed for translocation and biosynthesis, accounts typically for one-third of the energy stored by photosynthesis, leaving just 66.7%. Thus, combining the photosynthetic efficiency with the absorption and respiration factors gives an overall efficiency for the conversion of solar energy into stored chemical energy of $0.123 \times 0.8 \times 0.667 = 0.066$ or 6.6%. This is an approximate figure and many scientists give a lower value of about 5.6%. Under optimum field conditions 3–5% efficiencies are possible for limited periods, but typical annual conversion efficiencies are 0.5–1.3% for temperate crops and 0.5–2.3% for subtropical and tropical plants. These calculations are summarized in Table 4.

Table 4   Maximum photosynthetic efficiency of land plants.

Parameter	Factor
Photosynthetically active radiation/total radiation	0.43
Maximum leaf absorption	0.8
Maximum efficiency of absorbed light conversion	0.286
(Photosynthesis–respiration)/photosynthesis	0.667
Overall efficiency $= 0.43 \times 0.8 \times 0.286 \times 0.667 \quad = $	0.066

2.4   Primary production

The approximate global primary productivity broken down into land (or water) types is given in Table 5.

Table 5   Breakdown of global primary production.

Land type	Net productivity (% of total)
Forests and woodlands	44.3 (incl. 21.9 in tropical rain forests)
Grassland	9.7 (6.8 tropical; 2.9 temperate)
Cultivated land	5.9
Desert and semi-desert	1.5
Freshwater	3.2
Oceans	35.4

Most of this primary productivity is in the form of un-utilized cellulose, but its potential is yet to be realized since cellulose is almost invariably linked to lignin molecules in nature, and this lignocellulosic complex is very resistant to degradation.

Table 6 lists short-term yields and photosynthetic efficiencies of various plants, both C_3 and C_4, grown under favourable conditions of insolation, temperature, water availability, and nutrient supply. C_4 species cultivated in subtropical environments may yield in excess of 400 kg ha^{-1} day^{-1}, while in temperate regions a summer value of 200 kg ha^{-1} day^{-1} can be expected and occasionally surpassed.

These high short-term productivities however are rarely, if ever, maintained over the growing season, let alone over a complete year. Generally perennial crops with a continuous leaf cover capture and store the greatest amount of solar energy on an annual basis. In northern Europe a perennial grass crop or young evergreen forest can yield just over 20 t ha^{-1} y^{-1} at an annual photosynthetic efficiency of around 1%, while C_4 forage grasses like napier grass (*Pennisetum purpureum*) have produced 85 t ha^{-1} y^{-1} of biomass at an

Table 6 High short-term productivities and photosynthetic efficiencies of selected plants.

Crop	Location	Short-term high yield (g m^{-2} day^{-1} dry wt)	Photosynthetic efficiency (%)
Temperate			
Tall fescue	U.K.	43	3.5
Sugar beet	U.K.	31	4.3
Barley	U.K.	23	1.8
Wheat	Netherlands	18	1.7
Maize (C$_4$)	Netherlands	17	2.1
Maize (C$_4$)	Kentucky, U.S.A.	40	3.4
Subtropical			
Alfalfa	California, U.S.A.	23	1.4
Pine	Australia	41	2.7
Algae	California, U.S.A.	24	1.5
Sugar-cane (C$_4$)	Texas, U.S.A.	31	2.8
Maize (C$_4$)	California, U.S.A.	52	2.9
Tropical			
Cassava	Malaysia	18	2.0
Rice	Philippines	27	2.9
Napier grass (C$_4$)	El Salvador	39	4.2
Sugar-cane (C$_4$)	Hawaii, U.S.A.	37	3.8

efficiency nearing 2.5%. Examples of annual productivities are given in Table 7.

Of special interest for ethanol production are the values for sugar-cane and starchy crops such as cassava and maize. But most of the yields in Tables 6 and 7 are those obtained from agriculture where the end-product is a food, fibre or chemical not destined for energy conversion. Therefore whole plant dry matter yields are undoubtedly less than what might be achieved from an energy crop plantation geared to maximize primary productivity. It is also possible to harvest some forms of natural vegetation as an energy source, but not generally on a renewable basis.

2.5 Biomass wastes

Biomass wastes are organic materials for which no use has yet been discovered. Municipal solid waste (MSW) is an obvious example, but the term 'waste' is often used in a wider sense to include materials which have some value (for example, livestock manure and straw). These are more accurately described as residues than wastes.

Of all the crop residues available world-wide, straw is the most abundant at

Table 7   Annual productivities and photosynthetic efficiencies of selected agricultural crops.

Crop	Location	Yield (t ha^{-1} y^{-1} dry wt)	Photosynthetic efficiency (%)
Temperate			
Sugar beet	Washington, U.S.A.	32	1.1
Wheat	Washington, U.S.A.	30 (grain)	0.1
Barley	U.K.	7 (grain)	0.3
Maize (C$_4$)	Japan	26	1.1
Subtropical			
Alfalfa	California, U.S.A.	33	1.0
Sugar beet	California, U.S.A.	42	1.2
Maize (C$_4$)	Egypt	29	0.6
Tropical			
Sugar beet	Hawaii (2 crops)	31	0.9
Cassava	Malaysia	38	1.1
Rice and sorghum (C$_4$) (multiple cropping)	Philippines	23 (grain)	0.7
Sugar-cane (C$_4$)	Hawaii	64	1.8
Maize (C$_4$)	Peru	26	0.8
Napier grass (C$_4$)	El Salvador	85	2.4

around one billion tonnes. Its predominance can be gauged from the data in Table 8. At an energy content of around 16.2 GJ t^{-1} on a dry weight basis, the 885 million tonnes of straw would have an energy potential of 14.3 EJ, equivalent, on a heat supplied basis, to 319 million tonnes of oil. Though this is an impressive statistic, it is misleading as an indication of how much useful energy can be obtained from straw. Unless it is burnt on-site to heat farm buildings the straw would eventually incur energy costs for harvesting, transporting and converting into a higher grade fuel. In many circumstances the energy needed to perform these operations is so great as to make the overall conversion of straw to fuel an uneconomical practice. Economics too will often decide that residues, such as straw, would be better used as an animal feedstuff, a packing material, a building material, or for pulp and paper or particle board manufacture, etc., than as a fuel. There is a school of thought which believes that crop remains should never be harvested for energy production in any circumstances, owing to their value as either soil fertilizer or livestock feed. Clearly some compromise must be found between the two extremes of total removal and no removal.

Sugar-cane bagasse is an invaluable byproduct of the sugar industry for steam raising: the organic fraction of MSW is sometimes incinerated for use in district heating schemes; wood residues generated in the manufacture of forest

Table 8   Estimated availability of specific non-woody, fibrous raw materials, and estimated annual collectable yields per hectare.

Raw material	Global availability ($\times 10^6$ t dry wt)	Collectable yields (t dry wt ha^{-1})
Sugar-cane bagasse	55	5.0–12.4
Wheat straw	550	2.2–3.0
Rice straw	180	1.4–2.0
Oat, barley, rye, flaxseed and grass seed straw	155	0.5–3.5
Subtotal, straw	*885*	
Bast fibres (e.g. jute)	6.1	
Leaf fibres (e.g. sisal)	0.9	
Reeds	30	5.0–9.9
Bamboo	30	1.5–2.0 (natural)
Papyrus	5	20.0–24.7
Esparto grass + Sabai grass	0.7	
Cotton fibres	14.5	0.02–0.9
Estimated total	*1027.2*	

products are generally used within the industries themselves (making them about 40% energy self-sufficient); while sewage treatment plants also use the incoming waste as an energy source, digesting it to produce methane gas for powering works machinery. Table 9 gives the approximate quantities of organic waste produced each year in the U.K. In terms of energy content, one tonne of dry biomass is roughly equal to 0.4 tonnes of oil equivalent on a heat supplied basis, but only a small fraction of the potential energy will be retained in any useful fuel produced by a bioconversion process.

Livestock waste, from cattle and buffaloes, is an attractive substrate for energy production in the developing countries. Dung cakes are used for heat in many parts of Asia, but at a low efficiency of about 10%. This can be increased to 60% via anaerobic digestion to biogas. Of the world's total cattle and buffalo population of 1275 million, 20% are Indian. However, because these animals generally eat low amounts of poor quality fodder, their milk, meat and dung yields fall well below the global average. Around 220 million tonnes of dry dung are available each year from Indian cattle, or roughly one tonne of dung per animal. This compares with a U.K. figure of 3 t of dung per animal and 2.5 t per animal as a world average. These figures give an approximate world total of just over 3 billion tonnes per annum. In the intensive feedlots of the United States the dung collection efficiency is nearly 100%, while in the rural Third World it is nearer 30–40%. In any event, cattle dung is potentially a huge energy resource which can be enhanced with the dung of sheep, pigs, and poultry and by human excrement as well in countries where religion allows – an example being China.

Table 9   Approximate annual biomass 'waste' in the U.K.

Biomass 'waste'	Quantity ($\times 10^6$ t dry wt)
Cereal straw	9
Sugar-beet tops	6
Pea-vining residues	2.3
Sprout residues	0.7
Other vegetable wastes	1.6
Subtotal, crop wastes	*19.6*
Forestry wastes	1.0
Sawmill wastes	2.0
Wood-processing wastes	1.0
Subtotal, woody wastes	*4.0*
Livestock manure	46
Human manure	6
Domestic waste	18
Manufacturing industrial waste	10.6
Estimated total	*104.2*

2.6   Energy farming

There is little doubt that well-managed energy crop plantations designed to obtain maximum total biomass yields per unit area offer the best opportunity for bioenergy systems to compete with other renewable energy supply systems on a large scale. Within such schemes annual photosynthetic efficiencies can be enhanced by improved species selection, reduced photorespiration, pest control, the provision of adequate nutrients and water, and possibly by atmospheric enrichment with carbon dioxide in enclosed environments. The striving for maximum organic yields is of crucial importance. However, there is a trade-off between energy and labour inputs and the net energy of the overall system per unit land area. There may come a time when, on further intensification, the energy going into the system in the form of fossil fuels, fertilizers, machinery, etc., will be greater than the energy content of the final biofuel produced.

Unless the grown biomass is combusted to produce heat, the overall biomass-to-fuel system will consist of two main stages: an agricultural stage to grow the crop followed by a conversion stage to change the biomass into a gross fuel product. In most systems the energy crop plantation will deliver ten or more times as many units of chemical energy as photosynthate as are used as fossil fuel energy inputs. With lower levels of intensification, and where renewable energy or labour substitutes for non-renewable energy inputs, this ratio becomes even more favourable. It is the subsequent conversion to fuels that reduces the energy out: energy in ratio – sometimes to a value less than one.

conversion to fuels that reduces the energy out: energy in ratio – sometimes to a value less than one.

To cut down on the non-renewable energy inputs to fuel crop systems, plants able to fix nitrogen or tolerate limited water supply and soil fertility or both can be grown. Additionally, renewable wood or water power, for example, could provide the major direct energy inputs to the plantation where these are freely available. Technologies for improving primary production with little or no extra energy inputs are also available. In silviculture (forestry), coppicing, the cutting down of trees periodically so that new shoots grow, is possible with hardwood species like the alder, *Eucalyptus*, poplar, sycamore, and willow. This practice removes the need to replant after harvesting.

Mixed cropping allows the cultivation together of two or more species out of phase with each other's growth patterns and serves to prolong the period of light interception by the increased leaf area exposure. The leaf canopy cover profile may also be increased so that upper leaves, adapted to high levels of sunlight, and lower leaves, adapted to moderate levels, can together utilize these differences to give greater total yields per unit area. Non-nitrogen-fixing crops can be grown side by side with legumes to reduce the need for nitrogenous fertilizers. Additionally, a plantation containing two or more species is less susceptible than a monoculture to damage by external parasites or predators. In the final analysis it is quite conceivable that mixed cropping for the production of foods, fertilizers and chemicals, along with energy crops within an integrated system will make more sense, in terms of land and resource utilization and overall economics, than energy farms alone.

Aquatic plants have several advantages over land species in that they require no irrigation or appreciable rainfall, water temperatures fluctuate less than land temperatures, light absorption can be nearly complete giving high photosynthetic efficiencies, and mineral nutrients are often plentiful due to runoff from the land. Algae and water weeds can provide the biomass.

In California and Israel algal-bacterial systems for solar energy capture have been developed over many years. At the same time sewage is partially treated in oxidation ponds. The large organic molecules in the waste water are degraded to small molecules like CO_2 and NH_3 by aerobic bacteria, which are utilized by microscopic algae. Oxygen in turn is made available to the naturally occurring bacteria via the algal photosynthesis. The whole process is summarized in Fig. 2–4.

Harvesting the algal biomass for animal feed or biogas plant input is however, uneconomic due to the power costs for centrifugation. Environmental control to allow the filamentous *Oscillatoria* and the colonial *Micro-actinium* to predominate and then be separated out through microstrainers is being attempted but the dynamics of algal populations are complex, making species control difficult. However, photosynthetic efficiencies are high over the year and the versatile algal biomass produced, while perhaps being an expensive energy resource, can also be used for food, feeds, fertilizers, drugs and colloids, as well as integral components of waste water treatment and waste recycling schemes. The algae act as energy savers, rather than energy

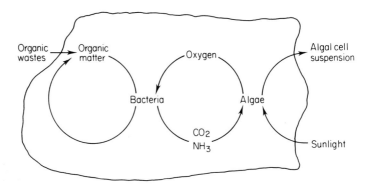

Fig. 2–4 Algal-bacterial growth cycle on waste water.

transformers, by replacing conventional processes dependent on fossil fuels by biological systems utilizing solar energy. The fast-growing water hyacinth, *Eichhornia crasspipes* has possibilities for aquatic biomass energy production in tropical waters.

3 Bioconversion Processes

3.1 Biomass to methane

The conversion of biomass to methane is achieved by anaerobic digestion. This is the bacterial decomposition of organic matter in the absence of air or oxygen to produce a gaseous mixture (biogas) of methane and carbon dioxide in a roughly 2:1 volumetric ratio. The carbon dioxide can be removed to leave substitute natural gas (SNG) of pipeline quality, while the residual sludge retains its nitrogen to yield a good quality fertilizer. It is a versatile process which can convert a wide range of raw material inputs from animal manure to municipal solid waste (MSW), algae, water weeds and crop residues; its reaction temperature can be maintained in the mesophilic region of 35–37°C or at 55°C for faster thermophilic rates; the type of fermentation selected may be batch, semi-continuous, or continuous. Its practice extends from large urban sewage works with digestion tanks of over 3000 m^3 capacity down to the 3–4 m^3 Gobar vessels of rural India. Though anaerobic digesters (biogas plants) can be operated on farms and in waste treatment plants in temperate climes, they are most beneficial to the poor rural dweller in tropical countries.

Two basic designs of small-scale biogas plants are in existence: the constant volume/variable pressure 'Chinese' model and the variable volume/constant pressure 'Indian' type (Fig. 3–1). The former is used primarily as a fertilizer production unit (making use of the digested sludge) and the input feed tends to be a mixture of dung (including human faeces) and vegetable matter, while the Indian design aims for good gas yields from mainly animal manure and the gas is collected in a floating drum. Both types are sunk into underground pits to minimize heat loss. To obtain high methane output it is important that the carbon/nitrogen ratio of the input slurry feed is approximately 30:1. Excess nitrogen might mean the presence of ammonia at a level toxic to the indigenous methanogenic bacteria, while insufficient nitrogen will slow the reaction rate owing to nitrogen deficiency.

3.1.1 Microbial biochemistry

The principles under which biogas plants operate are similar to those occurring in the gut of ruminants like the cow. Yet the details of methanogenesis within the biogas plant are by no means fully understood. Organic matter is degraded by a mixed population of bacteria under anaerobic conditions, with the formation of methane ($\approx 65\%$) and carbon dioxide ($\approx 35\%$). This overall process requires a sequence of four consecutive events. Primary hydrolysis involves the enzymatic conversion of insoluble organic compounds, such as cellulose by cellulase enzymes, to soluble organics. Secondly comes the fermentation of the stage one end-products

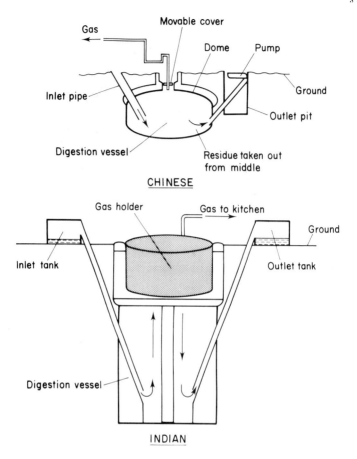

Fig. 3–1 Design features of Chinese and Indian biogas plants.

(carbohydrates, protein, lipids, alcohols, etc.) by non-methanogenic organisms to organic acids, predominantly acetic and propionic, as well as to hydrogen. The acids are then converted in the third stage by methanogenic bacteria into dissolved methane and carbon dioxide, which themselves finally undergo transition from the liquid to the gaseous phase. About 70% of the methane is derived from acetate. The process is marginally exothermic, that is heat producing, but the heat generated is insufficient to keep the temperature at the required level when the ambient temperature is 30°C or below, and so biogas plants work best in warm climates. The ideal pH for rapid methanogenesis is pH 7–7.2, though pH 6–7.6 is adequate.

Several of the bacteria involved have yet to be positively identified. Lack of knowledge in this respect has been linked to the inability to obtain pure cultures. Recently, however, acetate-splitting methanogenic bacteria have been isolated in pure culture. Four bacteria, the rod-shaped *Methano-bacterium soehngeii* and the coccoid *Methanosarcina methanica, Methanosarcina barkeri,* and *Methanococcus mazei* have apparently been identified as fermenting the key intermediate, acetate to methane and carbon dioxide.

The four processes are all slow and the residence time within digesters can be several weeks. This dictates the size (volume) needed to handle a given amount of waste feed. A faster overall reaction rate would reduce equipment size and capital costs. The methanogenic step is usually considered to be rate-limiting, but experiments suggest that the rate-limiting stage is associated with the final mass transfer in which dissolved methane and carbon dioxide enter the gas phase. As understanding of the processes within anaerobic digesters improves, particularly with respect to the factors that control the rate at which they proceed, progress towards a reduction in the volume/unit throughput can be expected.

In general, the overall reaction of converting organic matter into carbon dioxide can be represented as follows

$$C_nH_aO_b +$$
$$[(4n - a - 2b)/4]H_2O \rightarrow [(4n - a + 2b)/8]CO_2 + [(4n + a - 2b)/8]CH_4$$

When cellulose is the starting point this general equation becomes

$$(C_6H_{10}O_5)_n + nH_2O \rightarrow 3nCO_2 + 3nCH_4$$

The key methanogenic reaction is $CH_3COOH \rightarrow CH_4 + CO_2$

3.1.2 Substrates and fermentation conditions

Although cattle manure is the most commonly used substrate, lesser amounts are also available from humans, pigs, poultry, etc. At 15°C mean temperature, 0.18 m^3 of gas kg^{-1} day^{-1} dry manure is expected, which rises to 0.32 m^3 at 23°C. The energy value of the gas is normally 20–25 MJ m^{-3}. The rate of reaction depends on a range of parameters including plant design, operating conditions, raw materials, feed composition, *inter alia.* Temperature is particularly important.

Anaerobic digestion is by no means confined to agricultural situations. Figure 3–2 shows an operating scheme for the methanogenesis of urban waste in which digestible and non-digestible material are initially reduced in size and separated so that metals, glass, etc., can be reclaimed. The light organic digestible fraction, mixed with sewage sludge, passes on to digester tanks at 35–38°C, after which the carbon dioxide and hydrogen sulphide are removed from the methane gas. A typical plant gives an output of 4 TJ each day from an input of 900 t of municipal waste. The bacterial biomass is simultaneously recycled to the digestion vessel to maintain the reaction rate and gas generation.

In the case of algae, approximately 60% of the energy content of the cells is

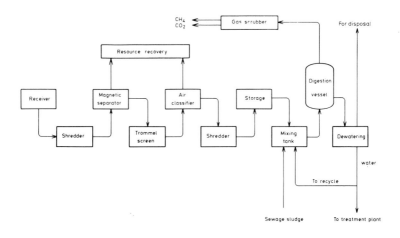

Fig. 3–2 Methanogenesis of municipal waste.

retained in the biogas following digestion; the remaining 40% is lost. This is a fairly typical efficiency for anaerobic digestion. Table 10 provides experimental data on gas yields and reaction times from the anaerobic digestion of several types of organic waste at 30°C.

Table 10 Gas yields from the anaerobic digestion of solid wastes.

Solid waste	Total gas yield (m³ kg⁻¹ dry solids)			Methane yield (m³ kg⁻¹ dry solids)		
	Total solids basis	Volatile solids basis	% methane	Total solids basis	Volatile solids basis	Half-digestion period (days)
Municipal sewage sludge	0.43	0.60	78	0.34	0.47	8
Municipal garbage only	0.61	0.63	62	0.38	0.39	6
Waste paper only	0.28	0.26	63	0.14	0.16	8
Municipal refuse (combined, free of ash)	0.28	0.31	66	0.18	0.20	10
Dairy wastes, sludge	0.98	1.03	75	0.74	0.77	4
Yeast wastes, sludge	0.49	0.80	85	0.42	0.68	–
Paper wastes, sludge	0.25	–	60	0.15	–	—
Brewery wastes, hops	0.43	0.45	76	0.33	0.34	2
Cattle manure	0.24	0.32	80	0.19	0.26	20
Pig manure	0.26	0.42	81	0.21	0.34	13
Wheaten straw	0.35	0.37	78	0.27	0.29	12
Grass	0.50	0.56	84	0.42	0.47	4

3.2 Biomass to ethanol

The anaerobic fermentation of biomass to alcohols, chiefly ethanol, by *Saccharomyces cerevisiae* yeast is a well-established technology. Yet its widespread use for the production of power alcohol is limited at present to the availability of low-cost sugar or starch feeds which need the minimum pretreatment prior to the fermentation stage. The more abundant cellulosic raw materials such as wood, straw, and newsprint require energy intensive, costly processing before becoming amenable to yeast fermentation. Revolutionary technological advances are required to make the bioconversion of cellulose to ethanol an economic proposition.

3.2.1   Biochemistry of sugar to ethanol fermentation

No matter what biomass source is used, in theory the equation

$$C_6H_{12}O_6 \rightarrow 2C_2H_5OH + 2CO_2 \, ; \, \Delta G = 234.5 \text{ kJ}$$

summarizes the process and shows that 180 units by weight of hexose sugar (mainly glucose) are fermented to yield 92 units by weight of ethanol – an overall yield of 51.1%. But in practice 47% at most of the fermented sugar is actually converted to ethanol. In energy terms, the free energy generated by the formation of two gram moles of ethanol and two of carbon dioxide from one hexose sugar gram mole is 234.5 kJ. Because only 67 kJ (28.6%) is retained as potential chemical energy the remainder of this energy is dissipated as heat. Thus, combining the maximum attainable photosynthetic efficiency of around 6.6% (section 2.3) with the 28.6% efficiency of carbohydrate fermentation to ethanol, an overall efficiency of solar energy conversion to ethanol of 1.9% is realized, though the practical efficiency would obviously be considerably less in a necessarily imperfect system.

For more information on yeast biochemistry the reader is referred to *Studies in Biology no. 140* by Berry.

3.2.2   Fermentation and distillation

Ethanol production can be carried out by batch, semi-continuous or continuous fermentations. The batch operation remains the most common. Nevertheless all industrial grade ethanol derived from molasses in the U.S.S.R. is currently manufactured by a modification of a continuous process. Productivity may be increased by 1–2% over the batch method, and the fermentation time is halved. On the debit side, sterilization procedures must be very thorough since the consequences of contamination are greatly magnified.

Figure 3–3 is a flow diagram for a typical sugar-cane blackstrap molasses batch fermentation plant, with a fermentation stage of some 100 000 litres capacity, in which the yeast seed stages are sequentially passed through increasing volumes. Commercial size fermenters of 2 million litres are not unknown. Following fermentation and separation, stills with highly efficient rectifying columns are used to obtain satisfactorily pure ethanol. These columns concentrate the volatile impurities in relatively narrow zones of the vessels from which the products can be drawn off as required. Ethanol concentration to around 85% v/v is achieved in a rectification tower, while the fusel oils are extracted in a separate vessel. Fermentations are dealt with in greater detail in *Studies in Biology no. 136* by Smith.

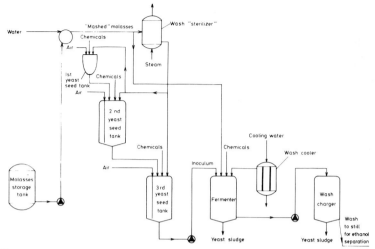

Fig. 3–3 Fermentation of sugar-cane molasses to ethanol.

The bacterium *Zymomonas mobilis* is used for fermenting alcoholic beverages in the tropics; it gives higher ethanol yields and lower biomass production than yeast does. A volumetric ethanol production of 120 gl^{-1} each hour has been achieved in a continuous cell recycle fermentation using *Zymomonas*. This is three to four times the rate normally obtainable from a traditional yeast fermentation, making the process both faster and cheaper.

3.2.3 The pretreatment of starch and cellulose

Starchy substrates like cassava, maize and potato must be hydrolysed to sugars, mostly glucose, before fermentation to alcohol is possible. The hydrolysis required is mild but still adds to the overall cost and reduces the net energy of the system. Mineral acids can be used under steam pressure, but with the disadvantages of corrosion, low yields, and lower recovery. Fungal amylase enzyme conversions give alcohol yields of 80–85% of the theoretical maximum and may be commercially produced from aerobic batch cultivation of the mould *Aspergillus niger* at 28°C and pH 4.5 for seven days. The subsequent hydrolysis stage is completed in 60 hours at pH 4.5 and 50°C within an agitated vessel, followed by fermentation of the glucose formed to ethanol. Cellulose is less readily hydrolysed than starch. Moreover, cellulose, along with hemicellulose, is generally protected from enzyme attack by a three-dimensional lignin polymer sheath which makes the whole lignocellulosic complex relatively refractory to bioconversion. Fungi such as *Pleurotus ostreatus* and *Sporotrichum pulverulentum* secrete enzyme complexes which can delignify substrates like straw and wood, but reaction rates are slow.

At present, physical, chemical and biological processes either individually or in combination are used for lignocellulose pretreatment, adding greatly to the financial and energy costs of the overall conversion to ethanol. The principal physical methods involved are pulping, milling and steaming for decreasing particle size and reducing cellulose crystallinity. The energy intensive process of ball-milling has been particularly successful but is very uneconomical. Chemical pretreatments include acid hydrolysis, alkali swelling, and sulphur dioxide and solvent delignification. Acid hydrolysis, usually involving treatment of the lignocellulosic substrate with dilute sulphuric acid at 180° for three hours, as in the U.S. Madison process, is often favoured. Figure 3–4 illustrates a scheme for the acid hydrolysis of wood to sugars which can then be fermented to ethanol. The disadvantages of using acids are; the corrosion of the capital equipment, the possibility of the sugar decomposing, and, the creation of unwanted byproducts through the reaction of the acid with impurities.

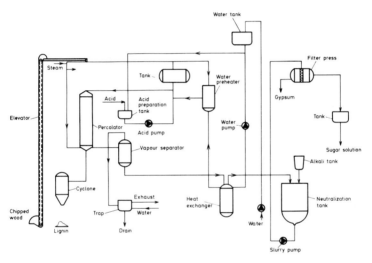

Fig. 3–4   Acid hydrolysis of wood to sugars.

The enzymatic production of glucose syrups tends to yield purer products than the physical and chemical methods, the enzyme is specific for cellulose and the reaction occurs under mild conditions, all resulting in higher glucose yields. However, the cellulose must first be released from the lignin sheath and so milling or other pretreatment is also required. Moreover the enzyme has to be produced (usually by the mould *Trichoderma reesei*) before hydrolysis can take place, adding an extra stage to the overall process. At the present state of technology, the acid route is more economical but less efficient than the enzyme route, and while there are no commercial plants yet employing the cellulase hydrolysis method, about 14 acid hydrolysis plants are operational in the Soviet Union and some in Japan.

3.3   Biomass to other fuels

Anaerobic digestion and alcoholic fermentation are bioconversions. These and the other main options are presented in Fig. 3–5.

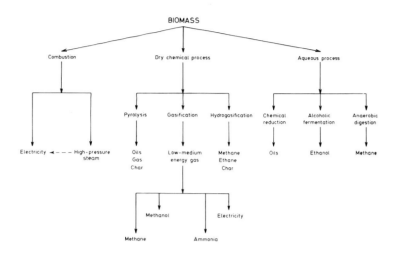

Fig. 3–5   Biomass energy conversion processes and products.

3.3.1   Combustion

The direct combustion of organic matter to produce steam or electricity is the most advanced of these conversion processes and, when carried out under controlled conditions, is probably the most efficient. Waterwall incineration, whereby water pipes within the walls of the incinerator are heated to produce steam at high efficiencies (the heat being available for district heating schemes) is gaining popularity. Co-combustion of organic matter with coal in more conventional power plants is also a comparatively new approach, while the advancement of fluidized bed systems for wood chip combustion is also now a favoured option.

3.3.2   Pyrolysis

Pyrolysis of wood in charcoal manufacture has been practised for at least 4000 years. The process entails the distillation of organic matter in the near absence of air or oxygen. Decomposition of wood begins at 300°C and is virtually complete by 450°C. The oil formed in all pyrolysis reactions is not suitable for refining and is also corrosive, but is useful as a fuel oil extender. Char production is particularly relevant to the Third World where it is often used in rural areas to provide a solid fuel with double the energy density of wood.

3.3.3   Gasification

Gasification is carried out in the presence of limited air or oxygen and at higher temperatures and/or pressures than pyrolysis. Where oxygen only is admitted to the reactor the initial product is a hydrogen/carbon monoxide mixture, but oxidation using air leads to 42% nitrogen in the mixture, thus lowering the heat value from around 14 MJ m^{-3} to the 7 MJ m^{-3} of producer gas. The Union Carbide Purox process for municipal solid waste treatment uses oxygen, the temperature in the combustion zone rises to 1600–1700°C, and the fuel gas formed has a net heating value of approximately 10.5 MJ m^{-3}. The percentage volume composition of the gas is carbon monoxide 45.6; hydrogen 27.3; carbon dioxide 12.8; methane 8.0; water vapour 4.7; nitrogen 1.0. As shown in Fig. 3–5 this low-energy gas can be the intermediate in a number of production routes. Methanation to SNG gives a product of energy value 38 MJ m^{-3}.

$$CO + 3H_2 \rightarrow CH_4 + H_2O$$

Methanol can be formed by condensation of the gaseous phase followed by distillation to 98% purity (see Fig. 3–6).

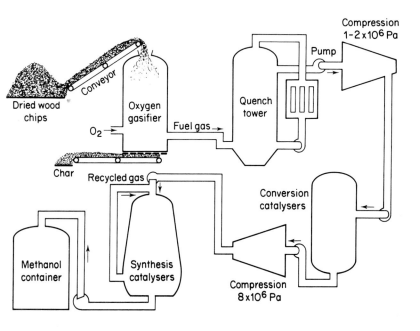

Fig. 3–6   Gasification of wood to synthesis gas and catalysis to methanol.

$$CO + 2H_2 \rightarrow CH_3OH$$

Ammonia, valuable in the manufacture of chemical fertilizers, is produced by conversion of the carbon monoxide to carbon dioxide, which is then eliminated to leave an almost pure hydrogen stream. Hydrogen is also formed by the reaction

$$CO + H_2O \rightarrow CO_2 + H_2$$

Nitrogen, obtained from an air separation facility, is added to give an $H_2:N_2$ ratio of $3:1$, which passes to an ammonia synthesiser, containing an iron oxide catalyst, at 475°C and 30.4×10^6 Pa. The overall yield from the reaction

$$N_2 + 3H_2 \rightarrow 2NH_3$$

approaches 90% of theoretical, with the unconverted gas being recirculated.

Electricity generation within a combined gas turbine-steam cycle is another alternative. Producer gas may become attractive in Third World countries as a source of work energy – particularly where the possibilities for biogas production are poor. In the industrialized world methanol can be converted at 90% efficiency to petrol directly using a Mobil process employing zeolite catalysts. Gasification is therefore a more versatile and potentially more useful process than pyrolysis.

3.3.4   Hydrogasification

Biomass can be converted to methane and ethane by reduction with hydrogen at 540°C and 6.9×10^6 Pa pressure. However, the need for high temperature and pressure added to the fact that hydrogen itself is a premium fuel limits the usefulness of the process.

3.3.5   Chemical reduction

This involves the reduction of aqueous biomass by chemical and physical means to yield fuel oils of varying compositions. Carbon monoxide, steam and a slurry of cellulosic waste have been reacted together at 250–400°C and $13.8–27.6 \times 10^6$ Pa pressure in the presence of an alkaline catalyst to yield an oil of approximate formula $(C_{11}H_{19}O)_n$ and an energy content of 40 MJ kg^{-1}.

3.4   Process selection

The main bioenergy conversion routes are presented in Table 11, along with the principal products formed and, where applicable, their energy contents. An important criterion in process selection is the biomass' water content which, if over 70%, may allow only aqueous processing without exorbitant energy expenditure on drying. The constitution and availability of the biomass raw material, together with constraints regarding land, labour and economics, are vital factors in the selection of the conversion path to follow and therefore of the efficiency that can be attained. Technological advances aimed at improving the overall efficiences of many of the bioconversion routes outlined are now being made.

Table 11   Bioconversion processes and products.

Process	Initial product	Final product
	Anaerobic digestion Biogass : CH_42 : $1CO_2$ $(22-28\ MJ\ m^{-3})$	Methane $(38\ MJ\ m^{-3})$
Aqueous	$\left\{\begin{array}{l}\text{Alcohol fermentation}\\ \text{tion}\\ \text{Chemical reduction}\end{array}\right.$	Ethanol $(19\ MJ\ l^{-1})$ Oils $(35-40\ MJ\ kg^{-1})$
Dry thermochemical	$\left\{\begin{array}{l}\text{Pyrolysis}\\ \\ \\ \\ \\ \text{Gasification}\\ \\ \\ \\ \\ \text{Hydrogasification}\end{array}\right.$	Pyrolytic oils $(23-30\ MJ\ kg^{-1})$ Gas $(8-15\ MJ\ m^{-3})$ Char $(19-31.5\ MJ\ kg^{-1})$
	Low-medium energy gas $(7-15\ MJ\ m^{-3})$	Methane $(38\ MJ\ m^{-3})$ Methanol $(16.9\ MJ\ l^{-1})$ Ammonia Electricity $(3.6\ MJ\ kW\ h^{-1})$
		Methane $(38\ MJ\ m^{-3})$ Ethane $(70.5\ MJ\ m^{-3})$ Char $(19-31.5\ MJ\ kg^{-1})$
Direct combustion of:	High-pressure steam	High-pressure steam
Wood chips $(18.6-20.9\ MJ\ kg^{-1}\ dry\ wt)$ Sugar-cane bagasse $(9.5\ MJ\ kg^{-1})$ Cereal straw $(16-17\ MJ\ kg^{-1})$ Organic refuse $(13.2\ MJ\ kg^{-1})$ Biophotolysis (see Chapter 7)		Electricity $(3.6\ MJ\ kW\ h^{-1})$ Hydrogen $(12.7\ MJ\ m^{-3})$

$(MJ\ x^{-1})$ refers to energy content.

Table 12 shows the present approximate overall efficiencies of the major conversion processes and also how the use of a specific dry raw material (municipal solid waste) gives a variety of process efficiencies dependent on the conversion route chosen. Aqueous processing via anaerobic digestion is less efficient than the dry treatments such as incineration and gasification. The efficiencies in Table 12 are based on the percentage of biomass input converted into fuel or heat minus the fuel requirements of the conversion process. They are therefore expressions of net energy yield. These examples, in terms of energy out : energy in ratios may be less efficient than the methods employed in rural Third World situations in which man-power and sun-power take the place of the fossil fuel inputs, but, being more energy intensive, they are much more effective with respect to rates of reaction and hence to the total amounts of energy produced.

Table 12 Bioconversion efficiencies (a) general and (b) specific for municipal solid waste.

| (a) Using appropriate* biomass input | | | (b) Using municipal solid waste | | |
Process	Product(s)	Efficiency[+] (%)	Process	Product(s)	Efficiency (%)
Direct combustion	Steam	65	Waterwall incineration	Steam	67
Direct combustion	Electricity	25	Co-combustion	Solid fuel	65
Pyrolysis	Pyrolytic oil, char, low-energy gas	45	Pyrolysis – flash	Fuel oil	37
			Pyrolysis– medium-temp.	Steam	44
Gasification (oxygen)	Medium-energy gas	60	Gasification (oxygen)	Medium-energy gas	62
Gasification (air)	Low-energy gas	50	Gasification (air)	Low-energy gas	45
Gasification (air)	Steam	65			
Anaerobic digestion	Methane	50	Anaerobic digestion	Methane	25
Ethanolic fermentation	Ethanol	30	Landfill	Medium-energy gas	20

* For combustion, pyrolysis and gasification – biomass up to 50% water content; for anaerobic digestion – wet biomass; for ethanolic fermentation – carbohydrates.

[+] Efficiencies based on percentage of biomass input energy converted into fuel or heat, minus the process fuel requirements.

4 Energy, Economics and Environment

4.1 Energy analysis of biomass energy

4.1.1 Net energy

Energy-producing systems require energy in order to furnish energy. Therefore it is important that the quantity of non-renewable energy input, per unit of energy output, should be minimized. Each input, whether as capital equipment or operational requirements (e.g. chemicals, power, heat, etc.), can be expressed in physical units per unit of energy product. These physical values can then be translated into the energy resource needed to provide them, so that each is attributed a Gross Energy Requirement (GER). GER is defined as the amount of energy source or sources which is used by the process of making a product or providing a service and is usually expressed in terms of megajoules per kilogram (MJ kg^{-1}) or, in the case of electricity, (MJ kW h^{-1}). Solar energy, by virtue of its continuous renewal, is counted as a free input with a GER of zero. Thus, the greater the substitution of renewable for non-renewable forms of energy, the more favourable the overall energy balance becomes.

The development of an energy source whose production consumes as much energy as it delivers would seem to be an unprofitable undertaking. However, some forms of energy are more effective than others, that is they are thermodynamically better fuels by reason of having the potential for a higher degree of 'available work'. Thus, a kilogram of fuel oil, combusted with a stoichiometric quantity of air, yields 42 MJ of heat. The same quantity of heat can be furnished by 1.5 kg of hard coal or 2.5 kg of lignite or 3 kg of wood. However, the heat derived from the oil is at a higher temperature than that from the wood, and so is more effective and can do more work. In some cases, therefore, it may be worthwhile to persevere with a bioconversion process which is a net energy sink but which produces a higher quality fuel than that which it consumes.

An important consideration with bioenergy systems is the net energy produced per unit of land area requirement, land being a constraining factor in a finite world.

4.1.2 Energy inputs for biomass growth

Costings and energy budgets have been performed at the Stanford Research Institute, California for a hypothetical energy crop plantation, in which the biomass consists of annual and perennial species selected for a high level of productivity at 68 t ha^{-1} y^{-1} dry weight over a land area of 4000 ha. The energy analysis has since been repeated with a similar result in terms of the energy balances involved; the data are presented in Table 13.

Table 13   Inputs per 272 000 tonnes dry biomass per year[a]

Major physical inputs	kg tonne⁻¹ dry biomass	GER : MJ tonne⁻¹ dry biomass
	$kg\ tonne^{-1}\ dry$ $biomass$	$GER:MJ\ tonne^{-1}$ $dry\ biomass$
Ammonia	16.680	844.0
Phosphorus pentoxide	0.840	5.9
Potassium oxide	1.680	16.1
Herbicides	0.050	5.3
Insecticides	0.025	3.3
Fungicides	0.017	1.8
Water	227×10^3	_[b]
Fuel oil (for herbicide, pesticide, and fertilizer application; planting, cutting, chopping, fresh hauling, turning, drying and dry hauling)	3.360	155.6
Steel[c]	0.240	21.8
Electricity (98% for irrigation)	14.34 kW h⁻¹ (e) tonne⁻¹ biomass	200.8
Seed production (0.3% of above total)		3.8
		1258 i.e. approx. 1.26 MJ kg⁻¹

[a] Gross energy content of biomass   =   17.24 MJ kg⁻¹
GER dry plant biomass   =   1.26 MJ kg⁻¹

Net energy gain in biomass   =   15.98 MJ kg⁻¹, which is 1087 GJ ha⁻¹ y⁻¹.
   Biomass energy output (17.24 MJ kg⁻¹) accrues from energy input (1.26 MJ kg⁻¹) to give approximately 14 units of biomass energy per unit of fossil fuel energy input (compared to the S.R.I. estimate of 18 : 1).
[b] The water requirement is put at 1500 mm rainfall equivalent per year.
[c] The steel is classed as a capital input with an amortization rate from 2–10 years, depending on the type of farm machinery of which it is a constituent.

In energy terms the findings are encouraging, but water deficiency can be serious, though it is not so in this particular hypothetical case. On a global basis it would appear that India and the Far East together with tracts of land in Brazil, Argentina, and Uruguay, and possibly the south-eastern United States and equatorial Africa have sufficient indigenous supplies of both rainfall and sunshine to avoid either reduced biomass yields or additional energy inputs.

4.1.3   Energy inputs for bioenergy conversions

The solar energy gained in plant photosynthesis more than compensates for the fossil energy inputs needed for an intensive energycrop plantation. However, during the conversion process of turning the biomass energy into a useful fuel the energetics are not so favourable.

Ethanol production in Brazil can serve as an example. Table 14 gives an energy balance calculated by the Brazilians for the growth and subsequent conversion of sugar-cane, cassava, and sorghum into ethanol.

The values include the non-renewable energy required to grow the crop and to ferment it. Also included are the energy contents of the crop residues, such as sugar-cane bagasse, since these can be used to raise steam in the conversion process. Not unexpectedly the sugar-cane route provides the highest net energy gains since saccharide materials require little treatment prior to fermentation, while starchy crops like cassava need to undergo mild acid or enzymatic hydrolysis. It is claimed that each unit of non-renewable energy consumed generates 8.5 units of alcohol energy starting with sugar-cane, and 5.9 units starting from cassava. These values may be possible by virtue of the combustion of renewable bagasse and fuelwood (instead of coal or oil) to raise steam, and by the fact that 90% of Brazil's 25 GW installed electrical capacity derives from hydropower. Thus the GERs for fuel inputs are substantially lowered, though added chemicals and the amortized capital equipment will still make a contribution to the overall GERs. Nevertheless, with 1 t of ethanol containing 29.7 GJ of energy and the calculated GERs of ethanol from sugar-cane and cassava being only 3.5 GJ t^{-1} and 5 GJ t^{-1} respectively, both conversion routes are clear net energy winners. However, there is some doubt as to whether the route via cassava is a net energy producer since the residues are not as readily available for combustion as is sugar-cane bagasse.

If cellulose is ever to be an energetically and economically attractive substrate for ethanol manufacture major advances in the pretreatment stages are required. Australian data, presented in Table 15, show which processes are currently the best net energy winners and which are the net energy sinks. All the raw materials used are primarily cellulosic with the exception of cassava, and it is interesting that the highest net energy return is from the straightforward pyrolysis of the fast-growing *Eucalyptus* tree. Anaerobic digestion to methane too gives a net energy gain, but it must be remembered that methane, and more particularly pyrolytic oil, are less versatile than ethanol as fuels, and especially as substitutes for petroleum.

From Table 15 it is also plain that acid hydrolysis of cellulose to sugar is less energy intensive than the enzymatic route. The adoption of anaerobic digestion technology probably provides the best opportunity for clear net energy gains.

The anaerobic digestion of municipal solid waste, 40% of which is normally paper and cardboard and a further 20% vegetable-derived matter and foodstuffs, has been practised for many years. Energy balances are normally very favourable with estimates of 1.6 units of methane energy output per unit of non-renewable energy input, increasing to 3.6 units out to one unit in, should the resulting sludge be incinerated and used for steam raising. The methane production scheme shown in Fig. 3-2 for the treatment of urban solid waste has a computed energy out/energy in ratio of 3 : 1. With respect to the

Table 14 Overall energy balances of ethanol production in Brazil.

Crop	Crop production (t ha^{-1} y^{-1})	Alcohol production (l t^{-1})	Alcohol production (l ha^{-1} y^{-1})	Energy (GJ ha^{-1} y^{-1}) Produced Alcohol	Energy (GJ ha^{-1} y^{-1}) Produced Residues	Energy (GJ ha^{-1} y^{-1}) Produced Total	Energy (GJ ha^{-1} y^{-1}) Consumed Agricultural	Energy (GJ ha^{-1} y^{-1}) Consumed Industrial	Energy (GJ ha^{-1} y^{-1}) Consumed Total	Balance
Sugar-cane	54	66	3564	78.5	73.5	152.0	17.7	45.3	63.0	+89.0
Cassava	14.5	174	2523	55.6	38.2	93.8	16.9	35.1	52.0	+41.8
Sorghum	32.5	116	3775	81.0	49.5	130.5	19.5	49.8	69.3	+61.2

Table 15   Energy requirements and net energy returns of biofuels production systems.

Fuel	Raw material	Process	GER (MJ kg^{-1} product)	Net energy (GJ ha^{-1} y^{-1})
Ethanol	Cassava tops* and tubers	Enzymatic hydrolysis/ Batch fermentation	17.3	+ 80
Ethanol	Eucalyptus	Acid hydrolysis/ Batch fermentation	105.0	− 452
Ethanol	Eucalyptus	Enzymatic hydrolysis/ Batch fermentation	> 105.0	< −452
Methane	Cereal straw	Anaerobic digestion	20.0	+ 7
Methane	Eucalyptus	Anaerobic digestion	20.0	+ 84
Pyrolytic oil/char	Cereal straw	Flash pyrolysis	4.8	+ 11
Pyrolytic oil/char	Eucalyptus	Flash pyrolysis	4.8	+ 131

* It is assumed that the cassava cellulose tops can be burnt to provide most of the process steam, but in practice this might not be possible.

methanogenesis of crop residues, this ratio has been calculated at 1.7–2.5:1, but non-uniformity of accounting procedures can cause problems when comparisons are being made.

In temperate climates digester heating is often required, especially in agricultural situations, resulting in reduced net energy yields. The following are U.S. energy balance figures (in GJ) for the anaerobic digestion of 237 tonnes of dry animal manure per annum:

Inputs: oil for heating and transportation 3.98; electricity for agitation, pumping, etc. 24.38; capital equipment 3.89; total 32.25.

Output: methane 42.71.

This gives an energy out:energy in ratio of 1.32.

At the low energy end of the scale, labour and solar energy tend to substitute for oil and electricity and so energy out:energy in ratios can often approach infinity. However actual energy yields tend to be small. In the particular case of one small Gobar gas plant with no motor-driven parts in the Indian state of Gujarat, an annual net energy gain of 79 GJ was made, which worked out at a modest but valuable 7 GJ (equivalent to just over one barrel of oil) per hectare-year for the whole village.

4.2   Economics of biomass energy

4.2.1   General considerations

In any discussion on the pros and cons of solar energy utilization it is important to appreciate that a change in the price of delivered energy to the consumer percolates through the entire economic system. Thus the costs of raw materials are also changed, as are the wages demanded by labour, the running costs of manufacturing processes, transportation, and so on. This effectively means that, since energy is required to initiate any intensified bioenergy system any rise in price of that input energy will necessarily result in an increase in the cost of production of the output biofuel. There is however a period immediately following a general fuel price rise when capital costs remain unaltered, and so a bioenergy system developed using these costs will gain an advantage over its competitor, the fossil or fissile energy source, because by the time the system is operational the energy cost of the competitor will have risen. These economic factors refer mostly to intensified systems since the utilization of unintensified natural vegetation as a fuel source in the rural areas of developing countries will remain largely unaffected by global energy price rises. However, the price rises still mean that the African villager will be able to afford less kerosene for lighting his home and the Asian farmer less diesel for irrigating his crops. Indeed, the OPEC oil price rises since 1973 have hit the Third World consumer hardest.

4.2.2   Centralized electricity versus decentralized bioenergy in the Third World

In the rural regions of developing countries the issue of centralized or decentralized energy supply systems is particularly relevant. Electricity is the most efficient energy source for lighting, but fully 75–80% of the inanimate energy demand of a rural community in countries like India is for cooking. In this context a centralized electricity supply is largely an irrelevance, even apart from the economics. At present only 14% of the households are connected up to a grid. 87% of electricity in the rural regions is used to drive pumps for agriculture, with just 13% ending up for domestic use (or 2% of the national output). A major economic reason for this is that electricity is subsidized for agricultural use, whilst the average Indian villager, who represents 80% of the country's population, cannot afford to pay for domestic electricity.

4.2.3   Intensified systems

Biomass energy would seem to be the main hope for many Third World countries to improve both their agriculturally-based economies and the lifestyle of their people — but what of the economics of the large-scale programmes proposed by some western and more advanced developing countries? The U.S. gasohol programme for converting mostly maize into a liquid fuel, ethanol blended with unleaded gasoline at a level of 10%, and the even more ambitious Brazilian National Alcohol Programme (Proalcool) are examples of these large-scale programmes. Costings for these and other biofuels production systems tend to be very variable, but it must be said that in general, at present, biologically-derived fuels are not economically competitive with petroleum-derived fuels. As far as the Brazilian operation is concerned substantial incentives offered to the motorist at the filling station are required to sell the ethanol fuel to the consumer. Estimates of the actual costs of production of ethanol from sugar-cane and cassava are hard to find, but at the beginning of the 1980s these were 17 pence l^{-1} for cane alcohol and 17.7 pence l^{-1} for cassava-derived alcohol. At the same time, the ex-refinery selling price of petrol was only 12.8 pence l^{-1}, but the retail price was 22.1 pence l^{-1}. Clearly the heavy taxing of petrol and the subsidies given to ethanol manufacture are necessary, but that is not the whole story. Brazil is only 18% self-sufficient in oil, with the shortfall being imported at an annual cost equal to half of the country's total foreign earnings. Proalcool aims to eliminate this huge dependence on imported oil.

Financial incentives have also had to be introduced to make gasohol attractive to the U.S. consumer as, in a free market with no incentives, petrol would still be cheaper at present. With the feedstock price for ethanol manufacture equal to 60–75% of the final fuel price many consider the gasification and synthesis route to methanol, using less expensive cellulosic feedstocks, to be the most economical way to liquid biofuels. Methanol from biomass would also appear to be more competitive than the use of oil shale or syncrude from coal as refined motor fuel, though less competitive than methanol from coal. However, although plans have been made to construct methanol from biomass facilities no large-scale plants have yet been built and so costings are based on paper studies.

Since advanced bioenergy systems are still in their infancy it is difficult to judge their economic performance. U.S. estimates for a number of conversion routes are given in Table 16. The processes are graded as to their comparative cost per unit of energy produced, with pyrolysis of wood to char set as unity.

Table 16 gives some indication of the wide variations in costs perceived from essentially the same process operating in different situations. It must also be remembered when making comparisons that a joule of ethanol or electricity is more valuable thermodynamically than a joule of charcoal and Table 16 by no means provides the full picture. Also some potentially attractive processes like the conversion of sewage to methane and of municipal and other solid wastes to methane or synthesis gas are not included. Where waste products are not used as the biomass feedstock the process is unlikely to be economically favourable in temperate climes. However, this is not to say that will it never be so.

4.3   Environmental, political and sociological issues

4.3.1   Environmental issues

Overdependence on wood in the rural Third World has already resulted in disastrous environmental consequences whereby removal of the natural tree cover has led to large-scale soil erosion during a monsoon season.

Deforestation often results in the decreased ability of land to retain soil, nutrients and water. This in turn can lead on to an often irreversible decrease in the ability to support plant life and the insidious process known as desertification. For example, in the Sahel region of North Africa the Sahara is spreading southwards, relentlessly devouring more and more productive land, while in northern India huge floods have occurred where rivers have been silted

Table 16   Comparative costs for various biomass conversions per unit of energy output.

Process	Comparative cost rating
Wood to char and oil for direct combustion	1–1.3
Steam production from wood via direct combustion	1.1–1.2
Medium-energy gas production from cattle manure via anaerobic digestion	1.5–3.3
Wood to oil via catalytic liquefaction	2.0
Substitute natural gas production from cattle manure via anaerobic digestion	2.2–5.3
Substitute natural gas production from wood gasification (oxygen blown reactor)	2.4–2.9
Wood to methanol via gasification (oxygen blown reactor)	2.9–3.7
Ammonia from wood via gasification (oxygen blown reactor)	3.3–7.0
Wheat straw to medium-energy gas via anaerobic digestion	4.9–8.8
Electricity generation from wood via direct combustion	6.1–6.9
Algae to ethanol via acid hydrolysis and fermentation	7.0–9.9
Corn straw to ethanol via enzymatic hydrolysis and fermentation	7.4–16.2
Kelp to substitute natural gas via anaerobic digestion	7.7–8.3
Sugar-cane to ethanol via fermentation	11.9
Wheat straw to ethanol via enzymatic hydrolysis and fermentation	19.5

up by soil washed down from the mountain slopes. The increasing scarcity of fuelwood can now necessitate a round trip of 50 km in some parts of Asia and Sahelian Africa for families in search of fuel. The alternatives are to move on to new land or to start burning more livestock manure for energy. This latter course in turn depletes the soil of essential nutrients and makes crop growing even more difficult. Many countries are now embarking on re-afforestation programmes, but forests do not grow overnight and the task of renovation on such an enormous scale is daunting. It should be stressed though that deforestation is not confined to developing countries since all over the world the clearing of forests to make way for farming land or for other purposes is a common occurrence. It is estimated that 245 000 km² (approximately the size of Great Britain) of tropical forests alone are lost in this way each year.

The planting of energy tree plantations is one way of replenishing forests and satisfying the energy needs of the people, but the biogas plant also has potential here, particularly in the rural Third World. Whereas the direct combustion of wood, dung cakes and crop wastes produces an unhealthy smoke, biogas burns with a smokeless flame, at 60% efficiency compared to 5–10% for open wood fires. It is also a more versatile fuel and is sound environmentally – killing most of the pathogens present in the dung input feed, and retaining the nitrogen, phosphorus and potassium valuable as crop fertilizer. In fact there is an environmental bonus here since twice as much nitrogen is retained in biogas sludge as would be available to the soil by direct dung spreading, in which over 17% of the nitrogen is lost through volatilization of ammonia alone. Thus a switch from wood burning to biogas burning where feasible in developing countries could be of great benefit to the environment as a whole – more trees left, more biological nitrogen fertilizer for the soil, more efficient and cleaner fuel for the home. Wood will still be a major fuel however, even if the potential for biogas is realized, and it must be remembered that wood burning can lead to air pollution. Certainly sulphur dioxide is not produced in any great amounts, as it is in the combustion of most coals, but a wood-fired power station, for example, would need to take some action in respect of carbon monoxide, oxides of nitrogen, unburnt hydrocarbon gases, and possibly some halogen compounds.

Finally we come to a controversial environmental issue – the so-called 'greenhouse effect'. This phenomenon results from the fact that carbon dioxide allows short-wave sunlight to pass through our atmosphere but effectively blocks the return of the Earth's long wave or infra-red radiation back into space. Therefore as more and more carbon dioxide is emitted as a result of increased fossil fuel combustion its build up in the atmosphere causes the Earth's temperature to rise. Warmer Earth temperatures would greatly alter the world's agricultural regions, weather patterns, coastlines, and even wealth distribution. It has been variously estimated that, with greater and greater fossil fuel burning, the atmospheric concentration of carbon dioxide will have risen by 300–700% by the year 2200. This compares with a smaller but significant rise of 15% over the last hundred years. The best way to deal with the greenhouse threat (though some scientists maintain that the threat does not exist) would be to drastically cut down on fossil fuel use as our main energy supply and insist on non-carbon dioxide-producing alternatives. This may well happen anyway, but the planting of more and more trees which, of course, utilize carbon dioxide in photosynthesis, will aid in carbon dioxide mopping-up operations and at the same time provide a fuel source which, when combusted, releases only the amount of carbon dioxide which it fixed from the atmosphere originally.

4.3.2   Socio-political issues

A modest-sized well-maintained and organized energy-tree plantation close to a village will eliminate much of the drudgery of wood collection. In tandem with such a plantation could come the installation of improved, more efficient stoves or 'chulas' which can cut wood demand for cooking by half and which can be fitted with a chimney to conduct smoke out of the house. These stoves would again reduce the time spent gathering wood and also prevent the irritation to lungs and eyes, leading to disease, which a smoky environment inevitably brings to rural Third World dwellers. However, smoke from wood-stoves does deter insects from entering the house and so the householders might be loath to have the smoke eliminated altogether. In cases such as these the careful application of pesticides might be the answer.

The use of biogas largely obviates the need for time-consuming wood collection, but again there are problems. For instance, only the wealthiest 10–12% of rural householders in India can actually benefit from the small family-sized plants, which require the dung input from three to five cattle to be effective. Many Indians are too poor to own this number of animals and so the answer for them should lie in the construction of much larger community biogas plants in which gas and fertilizer can be apportioned to the consumer by the amount of dung he can provide. However, although there is a definite economy of scale involved when installing a community plant, greater skills for operation and maintenance are also required, as well as a certain amount of community spirit. This is not always forthcoming in India where a fairly rigid caste system still prevails, and where the lowest caste, the Harijan 'Untouchables' might find difficulty in being accepted into such a community-based organization. There are also taboos in India concerning the use of human excrement in biogas plants, but it is to be hoped that this situation will alter in the near future. Human manure is already an important constituent of the input feed to the biogas plants of China.

Perhaps the most controversial issue surrounding the development of large-scale bioenergy production systems is in the competition for good quality land between fuel crops and food crops, and also the moral consequences of converting food crops into fuel. The Brazilian National Alcohol Programme has come under attack for concentrating on sugar-cane as its main substrate, since the sugar-cane needs to be grown on good soil which could be used for planting food crops. In 1975 two-thirds of Brazil's population had an insufficiently nourishing diet, yet the Government's 1985 alcohol production target will require the sequestration of the equivalent of 10% of the whole country's cropland. Furthermore large areas of forests have been cleared and unique ecosystems destroyed in the quest for land suitable for growing fuel crops. There is also an unpleasant human factor involved since small farmers have had their land taken over and been driven to the big cities where they inevitably end up destitute. These are not arguments against growing fuel crops for ethanol production, but they do draw attention to the need for formulating an all-encompassing policy, taking into account the social, environmental and political repercussions as well as the economic and technological factors. Furthermore, since many of the crop residues are combusted to save fossil fuel it is important that the nutrients removed are returned to the soil so as to make the programme sustainable. The other major biomass programme where the food versus fuel controversy has been raised is that of U.S. gasohol production from maize. Unlike the situation in Brazil which affects only the Brazilians, over one hundred countries in the world today rely upon North American grain for part of their food intake. Yet as the world's population grows world food production per person will eventually begin to decrease and the level of North American grain exports will be insufficient to meet the demand. In 1960 total grain reserves could satisfy world demand for 102 days; in 1980 they could do so for only 40 days. Almost half of the world's corn grain is produced in the United States, so what are the implications of diverting some of it to ethanol manufacture? Certainly damaged crops could have an outlet here and thus make good to the farmer some of his lost revenue, but contrary to popular belief the bulk of maize produced in the United States is used for animal feed.

Nevertheless, the U.S. target of ethanol production for 1981 would have required the output of nearly one million hectares of farmland, representing 5% of U.S. maize exports at five million tonnes – a considerable quantity. Plans for developing ethanol programmes are also underway in other major food-exporting countries such as Australia, New Zealand and South Africa and so the price of cereals may rise as a result. The repercussions are that livestock feeding and human eating habits could change worldwide, with the inevitable results that the poorest countries will suffer the most – as they did with the oil crisis sparked off by the OPEC price rises of the 1970s. The hard-liners will be out to make maximum profits nonetheless and it is disturbing to read one American view regarding excess maize that 'although the moral solution would be to use the surplus to fight world hunger, the economic and political facts of life frequently require other alternatives'.

Politics permeates throughout man's activities and especially those on a national scale and there is no escape from this fact. Indeed, the Brazilian National Alcohol Programme is a response not only to the economic pressures brought about by Brazil's £90 billion foreign debt and the fact that it wished to reduce its oil imports, but also to the need for some kind of insurance policy against the economic and political muscle of OPEC countries with their ability to cut production and raise oil prices. The sagacious management and deployment of 'home-grown' biofuels does give those countries prepared to invest in them a certain degree of energy independence. However, those countries that are able to embark on large grandiose schemes would be advised to consider all the attendant consequences beforehand, and not just the technical feasibility.

4.4   Integrated systems

Although we have looked at bioenergy production systems operating largely in isolation, they are best deployed within integrated systems of food, feed, fibre and fertilizer production, allied to improvements in environmental quality and waste treatment processes. Integrated systems invariably act synergistically and increase overall productivity over and above that which would be obtained from the sum of the component systems operating on their own. The concept is based on the minimization of waste and the maximization of energy and materials production with an emphasis on recycling.

Figure 4-1 shows an integrated system aimed at self-reliance for a family living in the rural Third World. In the diagram a biogas generator (represented by 'anaerobic fermentation') and algal growth system act as the fulcra around which the various constituent subsystems revolve. The algae, in symbiotic association with degradative bacteria, utilize waste products from various sources within the system and upgrade them to algal cellular matter which may be used as food, fuel or fertilizer. Simultaneously the incoming waste water is purified and can then be recycled. In addition to utilizing algae, water hyacinths and other under-utilized biomass resources can also be introduced, while further subsystems may also be added on. These could include an

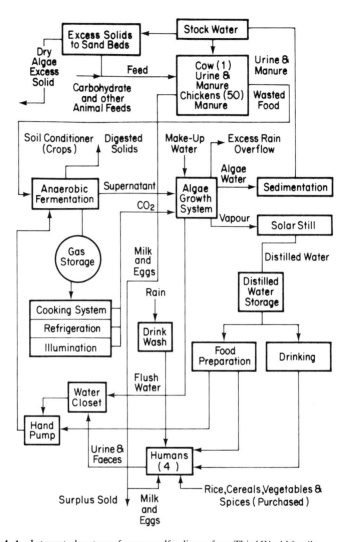

Fig. 4–1 Integrated system of energy self-reliance for a Third World family.

aquaculture component for rearing algae-fed fish and a biofertilizer component for increasing the nitrogen budget of the soil by growing free-living nitrogen-fixing algae and bacterial/legume symbiotic associations.

Another scheme, suitable for the urban Third World or warm areas of the developed world, is presented as Fig. 4-2. The two subsystems are geared to (a) photosynthesis and algal productivity and (b) methane generation respectively. The methane emanating from the anaerobic digestion of the algal biomass is envisaged to act as an auxiliary fuel supply for a principally fossil fuel-fired steam-electric power plant. Within this system solar energy is

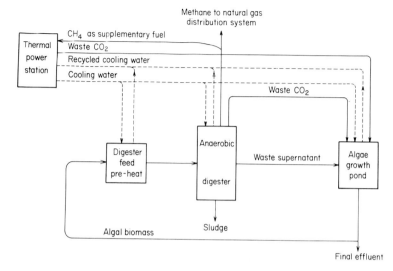

Fig. 4–2 Integrated system for biological fuels production.

converted into biological energy, methane energy and ultimately electrical energy. Emphasis is placed on waste recovery and recycling. For instance, waste carbon dioxide and cooling water are recycled from the power plant, to the algal cultivation pond in the case of the former and to the pond and anaerobic digester in that of the latter. The carbon dioxide aids photosynthesis, while the water is utilized to maintain the optimum temperatures for methane generation and algal growth. Waste supernatant containing valuable nutrients is recycled from the digester to the pond along with waste carbon dioxide to aid algal productivity, while the cooling water is also recycled from the digester to the power station condenser. The primary source of nutrients for algal growth, too, could well be derived from waste waters.

5 Bioenergy in Developed Economies

5.1 Present production and consumption

Fuelwood is an important energy source in many developed countries, especially in the rural areas of those countries which possess extensive forests. In the European Community the highest proportion of total primary energy consumption supplied by wood is found in Greece at 8.7%. Other figures available are for Italy at 2.4%, France at 1.5%, West Germany at 0.3%, Belgium at 0.2% and the U.K. at 0.2%. Outside the E.E.C. the values for Finland are at 14.6%, the Soviet Union at 3.6%, Sweden at 5.6%, Canada at 1%, Australia at 1.4%, the United States at 0.4% and South Africa at 0.6%. When the use of organic wastes is added to the fuelwood contribution, the proportion of national primary energy consumption supplied by biomass increases significantly. Thus, Sweden's becomes 9%, Canada's 3.1%, the U.S.A's 2.1%, and Australia's 3.2% since sugar-cane bagasse powers all the sugar mills in that country. When the methane used to power sewage works, the wood waste burnt in sawmills, and the agricultural residues combusted or digested on farms are also included it is clear that biomass energy can assume significant proportions – even in developed countries. In many nations biomass provides a meaningful contribution to national primary energy supplies – often more than nuclear power for example.

5.2 Criteria for site selection

The possibilities open to a country for setting up a biological fuels programme depend upon several factors. Two of these are energy density (energy consumed per hectare of land area which is generally related to population density), and biomass productivity (net energy output per hectare per year). These criteria will be modified by climate, terrain, land prices, food import levels, etc., but generally the less intensively developed, less densely-populated countries have the greatest potential for satisfying much of their energy demand via biomass. In western Europe, for example, Belgium and the Netherlands have population densities of 317 km^{-2} and 323 km^{-2} respectively, while those for Sweden and Ireland are only 18 km^{-2} and 42 km^{-2}. While a high population density is favourable for energy recovery from urban waste, the quantity of biofuel production is small compared to what is possible from energy plantations. Therefore, it is large countries like Canada, U.S.A., Australia, Russia and the Scandinavian nations (except Denmark) where bioenergy has most potential in the industrialized world. Energycrop plantations could occupy large areas in these countries, with the conversion plants located centrally. On-site farm biogas plants and wood burning in the rural areas would also be feasible, plus energy recovery from urban organic wastes.

In the case of the U.K., we produce only about 50% of our food and less than 10% of wood products manufactured in Britain come from home-grown timber. Consequently, since, at current prices, a farmer or forester is better off financially growing food crops and structural timber than energy crops, the immediate future for fuel plantations in the U.K. is unpromising.

However, the cultivation of fast-growing species on marginal lands unsuitable for food production and the utilization of natural vegetation does remain a possibility, along with energy recovery from the wastes detailed in Table 9. A similar situation exists in most of the E.E.C. countries, though France, with a fairly low population density of 94 km^{-2} and a large area of agricultural land has better prospects for biofuels production than most.

5.3 Examples of operating schemes

Operating pilot, demonstration and commercial bioconversion plants have increased greatly over the past four years. In the United States alone there are hundreds of facilities transforming waste feeds and freshly grown biomass into a variety of energy forms using combustion, pyrolysis, gasification, anaerobic digestion or ethanolic fermentation.

A system which is gaining favour in the U.S.A. is that of methane gas recovery from sanitary landfills. The process is a bacterial decomposition of the organic fraction of MSW and occurs at disposal sites naturally. The gas formed, with half the energy content of natural gas, can readily be upgraded to pipeline quality, and this has been done at the Palos Verdes landfill in Los Angeles County, California. There are many examples of MSW schemes, some in combination with coal, in Chicago, Milwaukee, St. Louis, Connecticut, Iowa, and New York State; while heat recovery for space heating and cooling from waterwall incineration is practised in Nashville, Chicago, and in the states of Massachusetts, New York and Virginia. Other schemes include the Occidental Research Corporation's flash pyrolysis plant processing refuse to oil in San Diego, and the Tech-Air Corporation of Atlanta, Georgia's pyrolysis scheme for the conversion of agricultural wastes into solid, liquid and gaseous fuels. Farmers have taken to the anaerobic digestion of livestock manure. There is too a 200 m^3 biogas day^{-1} anaerobic digester, receiving dung from 350 cattle, operating in a minimum security penal institution.

Canada is also pursuing biomass energy. Government incentives have been made available since 1978 to encourage forestry industries to utilize wood wastes as fuel and for the construction of electric generators fuelled by biomass.

In Europe there are many facilities converting MSW especially into usable heat or fuels. Also, the world's largest agricultural biogas plant came on stream in 1981 near Munich, processing manure from 1000 cattle plus vegetable waste. Between 4000–5000 m^3 of biogas are produced daily with an energy equivalent of 2000 l of heating oil. There are plans for using the gas for electricity generation to be fed into the local grid and also for methanol manufacture as a transport fuel. Currently there are 45 operational biogas plants in West Germany with another 30 under construction. Biogas-generated electricity is also being fed into the Dutch grid from a farm at Jutrijp, while in northern Italy an installation supplying 15 kW of electrical power runs on the biogas output from 50 cows. The U.K. has a novel scheme operating at Colchester sewage works, Essex where methane gas produced from the digestion of the sewage is compressed and mixed in a 1:2 ratio with diesel to power diesel vehicles at a higher level of performance than before. Back on the farm, there are 6000–7000 straw furnaces operating in Denmark.

On the alcohol front, the West German Government has launched a programme introducing the German motorist to cars run on a blend of 85% petrol and 15% wood-derived methanol. The 900 cars, fitted with modified fuel pumps and carburettors, sell for 15% less than cost price.

Among the plethora of biomass energy schemes in the Developed World probably the largest is the U.S. gasohol programme. Economic factors affecting the feasibility of gasohol production are the price of petrol, the price of grain, and the value of byproducts from the alcohol manufacturing process. Practical issues are ethanol containing only about 70% of the energy content of petrol, its relatively high octane and antiknock capacity, and problems of starting, performance, and phase separation of ethanol and petrol because of water contamination. There are also difficulties of a legal nature associated with ethanol, owing to its use as a beverage. A 3 million km test has been organized for 30–60 Nebraska state vehicles run on gasohol to obtain a clearer picture of what performance to expect. Early in 1980 there were 12 grain alcohol plants in the U.S.A. producing 300 million litres of ethanol per annum.

5.4   Future potential

It is difficult to predict exactly how much of the energy supply to the world's developed countries will be derived from biomass in say 20 or 50 or 100 years time. Many countries now have R & D programmes centred on one or more areas of biological fuels production. Sweden is pressing ahead with research and development into fast-growing willow clones which can yield upwards of 25 t dry matter ha^{-1} year^{-1} and are ideal for intensive silviculture. A report published for the Swedish Secretariat for Future Studies states that by 2015 that country's energy supply could be met solely by renewable energy sources, 46% of the energy emanating from such forest plantations and a further 16% from marine plantations and organic wastes. Within the E.E.C. (excluding Greece) it is thought that crop and livestock wastes alone could annually give rise to 40 million tonnes of oil equivalent (Mtoe) by 2000. This is equivalent to 300 million barrels of North Sea crude oil. The E.E.C. could produce 50 Mtoe of biofuels with little disturbance to other agricultural output; this is equivalent to 4% of the Community's projected energy demand for 1985. This would entail the harvesting of some catch crops and includes the 7 Mtoe of fuelwood already burnt. Some 36 Mtoe is conceivable from energy plantations by 2000 to give a total biofuels production of 75 Mtoe. The Department of Energy's bioenergy estimate for the U.K. is about 120 PJ or 20 million barrels of oil per annum, though when all wastes are considered this value could be doubled. Furthermore U.K. agriculture could be self-sufficient in electricity through the use of biogas generators providing 17 PJ of electricity per annum. Total energy savings in agriculture could amount to 47% by realizing the energy potential of straw and other farm byproducts.

In the United States it is estimated that the percentage fossil fuel savings which bioenergy could make above its present contribution range from 1.9% to 5%. While biofuels are probably destined to play a minor role in U.S. energy supply for the next few decades, 3–5.5% of the total energy market could be taken by biomass by the year 2000, and possibly 10% or more is conceivable. As the annual consumption of energy in the U.S. is roughly 10 times that of the U.K., amounting to 75 EJ, the actual quantities of biomass energy involved are not inconsiderable.

The U.S. is expected to produce 5.7 billion litres of power ethanol by 1990. In the same year Canada hopes to replace 25% of its fossil fuel consumption by forest biomass energy, particularly from its methanol from wood programme, and expects that 42% of its transport fuel will be methanol by 2025. Two other countries with great potential for liquid biofuels are New Zealand and Australia, where feasibility studies are now well underway.

6 Bioenergy in the Third World

6.1 Present production and consumption

Africa appears to rely more upon wood energy than does Asia or Latin America, and countries like Malawi, Nigeria, Tanzania and Uganda derive 90% of their national energy consumption from this source. Charcoal is also a commonly used fuel, particularly in industrial processes requiring high temperatures such as steelmaking. Senegal converts 50% of its commercially marketable wood to charcoal, and charcoal is now being increasingly produced from agricultural residues as the 'firewood crisis' in developing countries worsens. Dung cakes are another major fuel in south and south-west Asia especially; though today much effort is being directed towards their use in biogas plants. The Brazilian National Alcohol Programme is the largest liquid biofuels production enterprise in the world.

6.2 Criteria for site selection

Clearly the scope for biomass energy in the Third World is greater than in the fossil/fissile fuelled infrastructures of developed economies. This is particularly true in the rural areas where 80% of the people live and where most of the available biomass grows. Each village has potential for setting up a 'rural energy centre'. The biogas plant is normally the technological hub of such an energy centre, but of course this only becomes feasible where access to sufficient livestock manure and/or other organic matter is possible. A modestly sized energy tree plantation is also recommended here to supply 'heat' rather than 'work' energy, so that more of the biogas is available for irrigation or electricity generation. Algae ponds might also be included for protein and biofertilizer production and perhaps waste water treatment. The major constraints to these projects being set up are insufficient rainfall, poor quality soil, lack of animals (for the biogas plant), an unfavourable climate (unusual in the Third World except in deserts and mountainous regions), lack of invested capital and sociological factors. When regional or national bioenergy programmes are being considered factors such as land availability, climate, terrain, degree of dependence upon fuel imports, ability to feed the local population, should all play a part in the decision making process. Many countries have, or are in need of, large-scale re-afforestation programmes, but a more contentious issue is how far a country with obviously limited available agricultural land for food production should go in its search for some degree of energy independence through the growth of fuel crops? The answer to this question in the end rests upon a political decision. One would like to think that where a country was unable to feed adequately its own people, any biofuel programme would utilize the crop wastes only, rather than either the food crops themselves, or (even worse) fuel crops which have displaced food crops. Unfortunately however this is not how governments always perceive matters.

6.3 Examples of operating schemes

Since wood, agricultural residues and cattle dung are so widely used in the Third World one could say that biomass energy schemes are operating already in every developing country throughout the world. However, since they are almost without exception not organized or managed and are inefficient to the extent that 90% of the energy is wasted in the final combustion process, they are manifestly not planned bioenergy systems. Furthermore, deforestation and desertification give testimony to exactly how disorganized fuelwood use is in the Third World. Forests are disappearing from the humid tropics in Africa, Asia and Latin America at an alarming rate of 11 million hectares each year. At last national re-afforestation programmes are now in operation in many of the affected countries like Nepal, Thailand, the Philippines, parts of India, China, and Kenya where some 3.5–5 million extra hectares of forests are to be planted by 2000.

Other countries have simultaneously embarked on biogas programmes. India has around 80 000 family-sized units, with mainland China having around 100 times more. The Republic of Korea, with 30 000 plants, and Taiwan with 7500, are two other countries where biogas has caught on in a big way, while throughout the rest of Asia, parts of Africa and a few countries in Latin America, the biogas boom seems set to take off at any moment. Other schemes are operating with different biomass sources. Gambia and Senegal both have power stations fired by groundnut shells. Rural energy centres based on biogas and modest firewood plantations are being set up in some Indian villages, while in Sri Lanka a large biogas unit is run within an integrated system employing wind and solar energy converters for electricity generation. The resulting annual production of 60 MW (electricity) is more than enough to light, and pump drinking water into, 200 homes, but at a high investment cost.

The Brazilian Proalcool programme, begun in 1975, remains the most ambitious bioenergy programme in operation anywhere in the world. By 1978 1.6 million litres of gasoline had been displaced, or 11% of liquid fuel consumption, and there were 50 'gasohol' blending centres throughout the country producing an 80% gasoline : 20% ethanol mixture. In 1979 there were 4000 vehicles running on neat ethanol (96% ethanol, 4% water) alone, rising to 200 000 at the end of the following year. Four million m³ of ethanol were produced in that year, displacing over 20% of the total gasoline. In June 1980 the number of additional distilleries which had had to be built totalled 198, with a further 73 under construction. These will give a total annual production capacity of 6.3 million m³. Through the distribution efforts of Brazil's national oil company, Petrobas, nearly all the country's 27 states and territories are now using the alcohol/gasoline blend.

Meanwhile Brazil is starting to export some of its knowhow and its technology – mostly to other developing countries with similar oil dependency problems. Those countries on the verge of setting up their own national alcohol programmes include Sudan, Thailand, Colombia, Mexico, Argentina, Kenya, Panama, the Philippines, Cuba, Papua New Guinea, the Ivory Coast and Saudi Arabia and Iraq. These countries realise their oil reserves are finite and so in the long term they too will require oil substitutes.

6.4   Future potential

In developing countries it is impossible to foresee future biofuel production and consumption patterns, though clearly the potential is enormous, much more so than in the temperate industrialized world. The Brazilians are fairly confident that their Proalcool programme will satisfy 40% of their gasoline demand by 1985 and 100% by 1990. In 1990 too 50% of the huge Chinese rural population could be using biogas for cooking, lighting, electricity generation, and powering irrigation pumps and rice mills; while the cooking needs in Indian villages could fully be met through the digestion of livestock waste in biogas generators. National studies of three developing countries: Brazil, Sudan and India showed that the first two could easily meet all their future energy requirements through biomass, but that the high population density and great demand on local natural resources in India would restrict this potential to about 40%. There are many countries in the Third World which in theory could be self-sufficient in energy through biomass. It may be that countries like Brazil will be exporting their liquid biofuels to the industrialized economies early in the next century, and there could be a reversal in the economic fortunes of many currently underdeveloped tropical countries with the ability to produce 'bio-alcohols' excess to their requirements. However they may have to wait for this opportunity because of competing technologies such as coal liquefaction.

7   The Future

7.1   Genetic and enzyme engineering

Many energy production systems mediated by biological processes, particularly those involving microbes, may be improved in the future through advances in genetic engineering and enzyme technology. Genetic engineering involves transferring DNA molecules, in other words genetic information, from one type of organism to another via a vector, usually a virus or bacterial plasmid. This means new combinations of genes are brought together so that cells acquire the ability to perform biochemical activities previously beyond their capability.

An example is the transference of nitrogen fixation genes (known as *nif*) from the N_2-fixing bacterium, *Klebsiella pneumoniae* to the non-N_2-fixing bacterium, *Escherichia coli*. This may lead to the development of staple crops like rice and wheat capable of assimilating molecular nitrogen from the atmosphere, so decreasing the need for expensive chemical nitrogenous fertilizers. However nitrogenase enzymes only function in the absence of oxygen and so it seems that the expression of *nif* genes in a plant of agronomic importance is still some way off. Similarly the conferment of C_4 characteristics to a C_3 plant in order to improve its photosynthetic efficiency is again very much for the future. However while genetic engineering has the potential to make great advances, initially it is envisaged that first existing microbial processes will be improved through more traditional methods and lead to increased yields, elimination of undesired byproducts, cost reductions through lower power, heat, and chemical requirements, etc. Later, novel industrial micro-organisms themselves will be developed which will bring together in one organism the favourable attributes of several.

Great advances in enzyme engineering have recently been made in the technique of immobilization of enzymes on solid carriers which permits both re-use of the active enzymatic molecules and recovery of the desired end-products. This improves the economy of traditional chemical processes since immobilized enzymes tend to be very stable and can be arranged in sequence to produce a flow process of chemical conversions without separation stages like centrifugation. This could have applications in the enzymatic production of ethanol from cellulose, or other substrates, where more than one fermentation is required in the manufacturing process. Finally, interfering in the metabolic pathway of plants by genetical or biochemical methods or even both could aid productivity. Both photorespiration and dark respiration in plants are wasteful as far as net primary production is concerned and there are ways, at least in theory, to reduce their effects. Levels of both could be decreased drastically by the genetic manipulation of plants so as to block specific biochemical pathways.

7.2   Hydrogen from plants

The nitrogen-fixing rhizobia/plant root nodule symbiosis whereby hydrogen is leaked from the nodules and atmospheric nitrogen diffuses in, has possibilities. Harnessing the gas could make a significant contribution to a future hydrogen economy. A potentially more practicable concept involves the genetic manipulation of the tree crown gall-inducing bacterium, *Agrobacterium tumefaciens*. A gall is formed when the bacterium injects a DNA-containing plasmid into a plant cell. Genetic engineering has already succeeded in transferring the *nif* gene cluster from *Klebsiella pneumoniae* into *A. tumefaciens* and so it should be possible to transfer desired biochemical qualities into the plant gall itself. A large gall could be induced along the tree trunk to sequester large quantities of the plant's photosynthate (as sugars) and, via enzyme engineering, produce hydrogen which could be drawn out at low pressure into a small plastic pipe. A forest of such pipes could then be led into a hydrogen main at a power output estimated at one watt per square metre. The biochemical engineering required for such a scheme poses formidable problems, and this example is only given to indicate the direction in which progress may be made in the twenty-first century.

Hydrogen production can also occur through bacterial fermentation, photosynthetic bacteria, and biophotolysis of water. In the first of these however the hydrogen is formed at a much lower efficiency than is methane, the principal fuel produced by this method (section 3.1). The most important hydrogen producing photosynthetic bacterium is the salt-tolerant *Halobacterium halobium*. It carries out photosynthesis utilizing a purple pigment, bacteriorhodopsin. This pigment absorbs photons of light and releases protons from within an enclosing membrane to set up a mini-electrical potential. The bacteriorhodopsin is more stable than plant chloroplast pigments, probably because of the extreme environment in which it has to survive. Other bacteria are capable of anaerobic photosynthetic conversion of organic compounds into hydrogen and carbon dioxide, and the Japanese are now looking at the economics of simultaneous organic waste disposal and hydrogen production as compared to methane production.

Biophotolysis is the biological splitting of water molecules into hydrogen and oxygen in the presence of light. This is accomplished by organisms such as the blue-green alga, *Anabaena cylindrica*, maintained, under conditions of nitrogen starvation, in a sustained catalytic decomposition of water by sunlight. In the absence of molecular nitrogen the enzyme nitrogenase liberates hydrogen from water instead of fixing carbon dioxide. The simplified equation is

$$H_2O \xrightarrow{\ light\ } 2H^+ + [O].$$

Hydrogen is also evolved by adding either extracted hydrogenase enzymes or a platinum catalyst to isolated plant chloroplasts. In the case of the algae average efficiencies of 0.35% (free energy of hydrogen produced per total incident light energy) can be obtained routinely and these can be increased 1.7-fold by intermittent illumination regimes. The isolated chloroplast technique has made steady progress over the last decade. In 1973 hydrogen evolution was at a low rate and lasted for only 15 minutes, but evolution rates and durations have now been increased 10–20 times. Hydrogen can be produced at a rate of 1 1 mg^{-1} chlorophyll per hour for many hours, and higher rates are possible over shorter periods under specialized conditions. Unfortunately the system is very unstable, though the immobilization of chloroplasts in calcium alginate gels aids stability. Energy efficiency values of 12.5% have been obtained by Hall's group at King's College, London using a biocatalytic system. To further stabilize the biophotolytic system, synthetic structures have been developed which mimic plant photosynthesis. This technique entails the use of a photo-electric membrane modelled on the membranes of the plant chloroplast and utilizing chlorophyll as the primary element for the absorption of light photons. Electricity or hydrogen are the end-products of such a system.

7.3   Petrol from plants

The *Euphorbia* are latex-producing plants, species of which grow well on arid land. The *Euphorbia* latex has a hydrocarbon content with molecular weights in the range 10 000–20 000 and so is similar to a crude mixture of petroleum. Possibly this latex could be tapped directly in much the same way as is rubber from the related *Hevea* tree. Economic and energy analyses show it to compare favourably with other liquid biofuel production systems, though perhaps not as yet against petroleum at current prices. *Euphorbia lathyris* and *Euphorbia tirucalli* have already undergone trials in California, giving annual per hectare yields equivalent to 20–25 barrels of crude oil, together with byproduct chemical feedstocks. Genetic engineering could increase yields still further.

Hydrocarbon fuels may also be extracted from the green alga, *Botryococcus braunii*, producing hydrocarbons of chain lengths C_{17} to C_{34} up to 75% of its own dry weight. Vegetable oils are also extractable from plants such as soybeans, peanuts, sunflowers, palm, maize, olives and *Eucalyptus*. Experiments show that these oils can be used either pure or blended with other fuels, like diesel or alcohol, to run diesel engines, though at present the economics are unfavourable.

7.4   Biomass for chemical feedstocks

The present day chemical industry is over 90% dependent on petroleum for its raw material, and as yet the processing of biomass into chemical feedstocks and primary chemicals is at a primitive level of development compared with that of petroleum and natural gas. At the moment there are about five major petroleum feedstocks: ethylene, propylene, butadiene, benzene and *p*-xylene from which a whole range of chemical products are derived: plastics, rubbers, nylon fibres, resins, polyester fibres, solvents, antifreeze, and so forth. Current fermentation technology can easily produce chemicals of up to four carbon atoms such as methane (C_1); ethanol, acetic acid and oxalic acid (C_2); lactic acid, glycerol, acetone and pyruvic acid (C_3); and butanediol, fumaric acid and malic acid (C_4), but the production of aromatic compounds is not yet a developed technology. Therefore, apart from benzene and p-xylene the other major feedstocks are, or soon will be, capable of being manufactured from biomass through fermentations. A key factor in a biomass-based chemical industry of the future will be the ability to utilise lignocellulosic resources. Should a breakthrough be made here then lignin, for example, could be used to produce aromatic compounds like phenol and benzene, while at the same time the cellulose-fermented ethanol could give rise to a whole range of transformation products like glycerine, linear aliphatic alcohols and alkenes. Also, a breakthrough in the cost of methanol derived from biomass would open up a huge segment of the chemical industry to biomass systems. There are many organisms able naturally to produce important organic chemicals in significant quantities. The green alga, *Dunaliella* can convert solar energy to chemical energy so that 85% of its dry weight is glycerol, while *Candida* yeasts can produce 70–85% of their dry weight as fats. Therefore the potential of a biomass-based chemical industry is considerable.

7.5 Farming the oceans and deserts

Annual primary productivity in the world's oceans amounts to some 44–55 billion tonnes dry weight. However this resource is so diffuse that collection and transportation costs on a large scale would be exorbitant. But the organized growth of marine algae in ocean waters (ocean farming) for conversion into fuels does have promise. The U.S. Navy initiated an experimental programme to explore the ocean farm concept using, as its biomass resource, the giant kelp *Macrocystis pyrifera* which grows prolifically off the California coast. The programme, which was carried on by the General Electric Company in 1977, centred upon the cultivation of kelp on a network of buoyancy control structures and supporting lines submerged in the Pacific Ocean over an 80 km^2 area at a depth of 15–25 m. To overcome nutrient scarcity the cool, nutrient-rich waters at depths of around 300 m were pumped up for use by the kelp at an estimated, if optimistic, energy requirement of only 3 kJ per tonne of growth. Photosynthetic efficiencies of about 2% would be expected, giving ash-free biomass yields of 75–125 t ha^{-1} y^{-1}. The biomass produced would then undergo anaerobic digestion to methane gas and additionally produce byproducts such as fertilizers, salt, and animal feeds. However, the project has aroused controversy and met with many setbacks, seemingly caused by insufficient planning and basic research. It is still too early to judge the concept a sound one, though in theory it does have possibilities. Work carried out at the Woods Hole Oceanographic Institute, Massachusetts indicates that marine algal growth systems are better suited for energy conservation schemes, such as waste water treatment and chemicals manufacture, than the more energy-intensive processes currently operating.

Approximately one-third of the Earth's land mass is desert or semi-desert, but this large area contributes only 1.5% to global primary production. CAM-type photosynthetic plants are able to thrive in arid zones but are slow growers. *Euphorbia*, the 'petrol plant' is a member of this group, and its potential for hydrocarbon fuel production was outlined in section 7.3. Other trees like *Cobaifera* and *Croton* have similar properties and search is now being made for other desert species capable of oil and/or rubber production at reasonably high yields. Over 30 such species have been selected for further investigation by the U.S. Department of Agriculture, and guayule (*Parthenium argentatus*) is considered to be the best multi-use oil and hydrocarbon crop today.

7.6   The role of biomass in the twenty-first century

Mankind will probably see even more momentous changes, both technological and hopefully sociological, between 1982 and 2082 than it did between 1882 and 1982. With the passing of the petroleum era, nowhere will the change be more profound than in the way twenty-first century man obtains his energy. We have glimpsed some of the possibilities already – the potential spin-offs from genetic and enzyme engineering; hydrogen production from plants; petrol pump plants; a biomass-based chemical industry; and farming of the oceans and deserts. Yet there is one crucial possibility which could revolutionize the role of biomass as a future energy supply. This is the development of biotechnology based on lignocellulosic materials. For the saccharification of cellulose to glucose and the further fermentation to ethanol it is important to know how the production of the involved enzymes can be regulated and increased for faster, more economical transformations. Already a single stage conversion of cellulose to ethanol by a bacterial co-culture is showing immense potential. Similarly, characterization of the enzymes involved in the degradation of the lignin polymer must be accomplished. This would then open the way for the cheap bioconversion of the estimated 100 billion tonnes of cellulose and lignocellulose produced in photosynthesis every year.

However we must be realistic and take account of the competing energy systems available to mankind. At present energy consumption rates, and if no additional reserves or resources become available, it is estimated that natural gas would be exhausted by about the year 2047, oil by 2080, and coal plus lignite by 2180. Uranium for use in thermal nuclear reactors would last until 2017, but nuclear breeder or nuclear fusion technology, if developed, would in theory, take us nearly to the year 40 000.

Yet the problem with the fossil and fissile energy resources is that as they are being used up they become increasingly difficult to reach and more expensive to extract. This will inevitably push the price up and so, in economic terms, alternatives, such as biomass energy, should play an ever-increasing role.

In the meantime it would seem that synthetic fuels made from coal will be the major supply of liquid fuels when the oil runs out. Shale oil and 'tar sands' may have a limited role, but in the long term biomass would seem to be one answer, probably in tandem with solar and/or nuclear-generated hydrogen. But biomass conversion has the advantage of being a proven technology now, and if the breakthroughs in lignocellulose bioconversion are achieved, then the future of biomass energy in the twenty-first century and beyond looks assured. However, since the time lags for fuel substitutions are great, it may not be for another 100 years that fossil fuels are superseded by essentially renewable energy systems. By that time biomass energy production will be playing a major, and probably crucial, role!

Further Reading

ANDERSON, R. E. (1979). *Biological Paths to Self-Reliance.* Van Nostrand Reinhold Co., New York.

BARNETT, A., PYLE, L. and SUBRAMANIAN, S. K. (1978). *Biogas Technology in the Third World.* International Development Research Centre, Ottawa.

BERRY, D. R. (1982). *Biology of Yeast.* Studies in Biology no. 140. Edward Arnold, London.

BUNGAY, H. R. (1981). *Energy, The Biomass Option.* John Wiley, New York.

CHEREMISINOFF, N. P. (1979). *Gasohol for Energy Production.* Ann Arbor Science Publishers, Michigan.

COOMBS, J. and HALL, D. O. (eds) (1981–). *Biomass –* an international journal. Applied Science Publishers Ltd., London.

EARL, D. E. (1975). *Forest Energy and Economic Development.* Oxford University Press, Oxford.

GOLUEKE, C. G. (1977). *Biological Reclamation of Solid Wastes.* Rodale Press, Pennsylvania.

HALL, D. O., BARNARD, G. W. and MOSS, P. A. (1982). *Biomass for Energy in the Developing Countries.* Pergamon Press, Oxford.

HALL, D. O. (1978). Solar energy conversion through biology – could it be a practical energy source? *Fuel,* **57**, 322–33.

HALL, D. O. and RAO, K. K. (1981). *Photosynthesis.* Studies in Biology no. 37 (3rd edition). Edward Arnold, London.

LIPINSKY, E. S. (1981). Chemicals from biomass: petrochemical substitution options. *Science,* **212**, 1465–71.

National Academy of Sciences (1977). *Methane Generation from Human, Animal and Agricultural Wastes.* NAS, Washington, D.C.

PALZ, W., CHARTIER, P. and HALL, D. O. (editors) (1981). *Energy from Biomass –* 1st E.C. Conference. Applied Science Publishers Ltd., London.

SAN PIETRO, A. (ed.) (1980). *Biochemical and Photosynthetic Aspects of Energy Production.* Academic Press, New York.

SLESSER, M. and LEWIS, C. (1979). *Biological Energy Resources.* E. & F. N. Spon Ltd., London.

SMITH, J. E. (1981). *Biotechnology.* Studies in Biology no. 136. Edward Arnold, London.

SPINKS, A. (1982). Alternatives to fossil petrol. *Chemistry in Britain,* **18**, 99–105.

Index

Conversion Factors

Energy units

1 exajoule = 10^3 petajoules = 10^6 terajoules = 10^9 gigajoules = 10^{12} megajoules = 10^{15} kilojoules = 10^{18} joules
1 megajoule (MJ) = 0.28 kWh = 238.85 kcal = 947.92 BTU = 0.37 hph
1 tce (ton coal equivalent) = 26.9 GJ
1 toe (tonne oil equivalent) = 7.5 barrels (North Sea crude) = 44.8 GJ
1000 ft³ natural gas = 28.3 m³ natural gas = 1.1 GJ

Area units

1 hectare = 2.47 acres = 0.01 km²

Power units

1 watt = 1 Js⁻¹ = 10^{-3} kW = 1.34×10^{-3} hp

Pressure units

1 pascal (Pa) = 0.102 kg − force m⁻²

Biology Dept.
King George V College